A Day
in the Life of
BILLY
GRAHAM

DEBORAH HART STROBER
GERALD S. STROBER

SQUAREONE
PUBLISHERS

COVER DESIGNER: Phaedra Mastrocola
IN-HOUSE EDITOR: Marie Caratozzolo
TYPESETTER: Gary A. Rosenberg
COVER AND INTERIOR PHOTOS: Courtesy of BGEA: Russ Busby

Square One Publishers
115 Herricks Road
Garden City Park, NY 11040
(516) 535-2010 • (877) 900-BOOK
www.squareonepublishers.com

Library of Congress Cataloging-in-Publication Data
Strober, Deborah H. (Deborah Hart), 1940–
    [Graham]
    A day in the life of Billy Graham : living the message / Deborah Hart
Strober, Gerald S. Strober.
        p. cm.
    Includes bibliographical references and index.
    ISBN 0-7570-0092-4 (pbk. : alk. paper)
    1. Graham, Billy, 1918– I. Strober, Gerald S. II. Title.
BV3785.G69 S87   2003
269'.2'092—dc21

                                                        2003008951

Printed in the United States of America

10   9   8   7   6   5   4   3   2   1

Contents

Acknowledgments, v
About This Book, vii

Introduction, 1
1. The Cincinnati Mission, 3
2. Beginnings, 25
3. A Day at Home, 35
4. Early Morning in Jackson, 73
5. The Morning Continues, 85
6. Noon, 101
7. Midday Agenda, 113
8. Toward the Arena, 125
9. Flashback to the Holy Land, 133
10. "Now Is the Hour," 143
11. The End of a Very Long Day, 163
    Epilogue, 171

Traveling with Billy Graham, 175
Books by Billy Graham, 185
Contact Information, 187
Index, 189

For our grandchildren

Ran Michael Benjamin
&
Marley Grace Sterling

Acknowledgments

The creation of this book would not have been possible without the support and contributions of a number of people.

For their unwavering assistance, unfailing courtesy, and genuine friendliness during the research of this book, we must offer deep appreciation to several members and former members of the Billy Graham Evangelistic Association, especially Dr. T.W. Wilson, Dr. Grady Wilson, and Dr. William Smyth, as well as Cliff Barrows, Don Bailey, George Wilson, Stephanie Wills, and Charles Riggs. A sincere note of gratitude goes to Mr. Graham's affable and efficient media representative, A. Larry Ross, and his able associate Melany Ethridge; their professionalism and good humor were impressive and appreciated. We also thank Russ Busby for his wonderful photographs. We would further like to express our admiration to all of the other people mentioned in our book, whose stories helped complete the book's message.

For encouraging us to undertake this project, we must thank our agent, Ronald Goldfarb. We also extend special appreciation to Rudy Shur of Square One Publishers for recognizing the importance of publishing a book such as this. And we thank Marie Caratozzolo for her skillful editing of our manuscript.

Finally, and most important, we are forever indebted to Billy Graham for his willingness and cooperation in allowing us to take this unique look into his personal life, and then letting us share it with the world.

About This Book

For more than five decades, Billy Graham has occupied a special place in the hearts and minds of millions of people everywhere. He consistently ranks as one of the world's most admired individuals—a man of vision and rectitude, integrity, and principle. True to his calling, Billy Graham's unshakable commitment to preaching the Word "in season and out of season" has offered hope and inspiration to countless individuals worldwide.

It is my good fortune to have known Mr. Graham for more than thirty years. We first met when I served as a liaison to the evangelical Christian community. And since then, we have shared a number of private correspondences. I have visited with him at his home in Montreat, North Carolina, and have attended several of his crusades and missions.

In my earlier works on Billy Graham, I focused on the history of his ministry and of his impact on society. In this book, I wanted to give the reader greater insight into his personal, everyday life. For this endeavor, I have had the professional privilege, as well as the personal pleasure, of being joined by author Deborah Hart Strober, my beloved wife.

To give the reader a unique comprehensive view of the evangelist's complex life, this book is based on actual events that took place over *several* days and spanned a period of many years. We accompany Mr. Graham on two crusades; travel with him to Israel, where he tours Jerusalem and meets with some of its residents and leaders; and visit with him at his home, where he conducts business, but somehow finds time to relax with his wife and true helpmate, Ruth Bell Graham. *A Day in the Life of Billy Graham* transports the reader through time and over great distances to see the evangelist during his childhood and formative years, watch the incredible growth of his ministry, and witness his personal relationships with people of all creeds and from all walks of life. At its core, this work consistently shows Billy Graham's unyielding belief that the power of God can and does transform people's lives.

Every crusade and mission led by Billy Graham and his evangelical organization has been inspirational; each has made an impact on the lives of those individuals who were either in attendance or who watched from their televisions. This book focuses on two. The first took place in Jackson, Mississippi, in 1975; during this crusade, I had the unique opportunity of accompanying Graham and his team, witnessing them as they met the inherent challenges of each day's grueling schedule. Being at Billy's side over the course of this crusade allowed me a view of this incredible man that was truly unique. And it is these first-hand experiences that make up the lion's share of this book. Over the years, Billy and I have remained in touch, and during the 2002 mission in Cincinnati, Ohio, Deborah and I were pleased to have the opportunity to greet him again. Deborah and I found it especially meaningful to focus on the services in these two cities for our book. Both cities have suffered from intense racial tension, and Mr. Graham—in addition to conveying his basic message of salvation through faith in Christ—sought to defuse this strife through reconciliation.

Today, although he no longer keeps up the hectic pace and exhausting schedule he once did, Billy Graham continues to live the message that is the heart of his life's work. As he has done since accepting Christ as a teenager, he remains a faithful steward, using his remarkable personality, intelligence, and communication skills to preach, to chair his widespread organization, and to counsel people from all walks of life as they seek to find peace with God. We expect that one day, Billy Graham will be told, "Well done, my good and faithful servant."

Introduction

It always comes as a surprise to me when a gifted writer and interpreter of our faith wishes to tell something about me. The "days" in this book are similar to many others. If anything has been omitted, it is the larger scope of the activities of members of my team, members of local mission committees, and, most of all, of the sacrifice my own wife and children have made because of my ministry.

I could wish that no one reading this record would fail to see the beautiful manifestation of the power and sovereignty of God in this ministry. As for me, I can claim no supernatural power of my own. There are many godly and talented men, but God has chosen me in his sovereign right to proclaim the message of salvation through faith in his son, Jesus Christ. Now this is a humbling truth. Therefore I find myself in the position of John and Charles Wesley, who took as a guiding passage from the Psalms, "Not unto us, O Lord, not unto us, but unto thy name give glory, for thy mercy and for thy truth's sake [Psalm 115:1].

—Billy Graham

At the 2002 Cincinnati Mission, a crowd of 63,000 listens to Billy Graham.

1

The Cincinnati Mission

IT WAS 6:30 ON THE STIFLINGLY HOT and humid evening of Thursday, June 27, 2002. As attendees filed into Paul Brown Stadium for the opening service of Billy Graham's Greater Cincinnati and Northern Kentucky Mission, the skies suddenly opened. Those who were not already beyond the entryway dashed back under its protective cover as the rainstorm ran its course.

A few hours earlier, Billy Graham sat quietly in his hotel room in the downtown area of the "Queen City," going over his notes for the evening's sermon. It had been a day of study, prayer, and rest. On the days he preached, Billy always anticipated the physical and, more importantly, spiritual stress of speaking to thousands of people. Sometimes he felt as if the devil himself was perched on his shoulder.

The evangelist's sense of responsibility has always been enormous. It was the mission's opening night, and Graham's first public speaking appearance in nine months. As always, he was very much aware that the weight of the eternal destiny of a stadium full of people could depend on the words he would utter in the next three hours. Having recently dealt with a number of medical issues, including eye surgery and a serious case of sinusitis that also required surgery, he knew that he had to summon uncommon energy to preach that evening.

As Billy reviewed the Biblical passages that were at the core of his evening's message, he recalled the last time he was in Cincinnati. It was during a 1977 crusade, as his multi-day missions were then called. Five years in the making, it had gone on for four weeks. Now in 2002, he had returned. He thought about why he had accepted the invitation to come to this particular city. After all, he had received many similar invitations in the past year, beckoning him and his organization to hold missions in cities throughout the United States. The decision to hold this mission in Cincinnati resulted from the evangelist's concern over the city's serious racial problems, which had intensified over the previous two years. Cincinnati's turbulent, often-violent situation first came to Graham's attention during the spring of 2001, when he had been holding a series of meetings in Louisville, Kentucky. Louisville was only 100 miles from Cincinnati, and its newspapers and other media outlets were filled with reports of the growing unrest.

Coincidentally, at that time, some local pastors in the greater Cincinnati area had begun to organize an effort to invite the evangelist to town. In October 2001, they embarked on a mail campaign in which Billy received more than 200 letters, inviting him to hold a mission in their city. For Billy, receiving those letters confirmed his belief that God was leading him there—that the Holy Spirit was saying, "Cincinnati is the place you ought to go."

VIEW OF THE CITY

A major metroplitan area, Cincinnati is the twenty-fourth largest city in the United States, encompassing thirteen counties and more than a hundred municipalities and townships. According to the 2000 census, almost 2 million people live there. In one major survey taken during the last decade of the twentieth century, Cincinnati was rated as the best place to live in North America. It has also been cited by *Fortune* magazine as one of the "top U.S. cities for work and family."

The city and its suburbs are home to eight Fortune 500 companies, including Proctor and Gamble, Kroger, Fifth National Bank, and Cinergy Corporation. The International Air Transport Association rates the Greater Cincinnati International Airport as the number-one gateway in the United States. The area contains thirty hospitals, including the world-renowned Children's Hospital Medical Center, and has numerous cultural institutions, including a symphony, ballet and opera companies, three major art museums, and a regional theater. It also sponsors the oldest musical festival in the Western Hemisphere. Just two weeks before the mission's opening, in the presence of First Lady Laura Bush and boxing great Muhammad Ali, the groundbreaking was held for the National Underground Railroad Freedom Center. This major facility, expected to open in 2004, will commemorate the nation's first human rights movement—the Underground Railroad, which provided networks to freedom for African-American slaves during the period of the antebellum South.

Despite these apparent achievements, a palpable sense of racial tension existed in the city. The African-American community regarded itself as the victim of both police brutality and official indifference. A series of shootings by police—the latest occurring less than three months prior to the mission's opening—resulted in the deaths of fifteen young African-American men since 1995. It had polarized the city.

An organization calling itself "Boycott Cincinnati" actively sought to discourage Billy Graham from coming to the city, winning support from a number of black leaders, including the controversial Reverend Al Sharpton. Upon visiting the city, Sharpton stated, "He [Graham] can see what kind of controversy is going on here. He doesn't need to get himself involved in that." Taking a slightly different position, the Reverend Steven K. Wheeler endorsed the boycott in a column in the *Cincinnati Herald*, acknowledging that some individuals felt "the Billy Graham revival will bring racial harmony and healing to our city." He cautioned, however, "Not every revival is of God." Wheeler concluded his article by stating, "The Lord is in this boycott and this revival will not bring healing. It will bring the illusion of unity, and when the revival is over, the White folks will go their way and the Black folks will go their way."

Although the organizers of the boycott had been successful in causing the cancellation of past events, such as the annual meeting of the Progressive National Baptist Association, they were not able to prevent the Graham Mission from taking place.

The Concerned Clergy, a group of twenty-four pastors that was formed following the April 2002 riots, took a more moderate stance regarding the validity of the mission. Reverend Clarence Wallace, pastor of Carmel Presbyterian Church and member of the Concerned Clergy, appreciated Graham's motivation in coming to his city, but claimed "the problems that affect Cincinnati are much more severe than Billy Graham understood." He conceded that the city's 2002 mission was more inclusive than the 1977 crusade had been; however, it could not be considered a "cure-all for Cincinnati." Wallace maintained that while the area's white clergy believed Graham could make a difference, the fact remained that their churches were largely suburban and not engaged in many racial issues. On the other hand, black clergymen did not have the same level of expectation as their white counterparts, and, as Wallace said, "They did not believe this could be a turning point in the life of the city."

Whatever the mission's long-term impact, the black pastors who were involved in the meetings were generally pleased by the African-American turnout, comparing it to the attendance at the city's 1977 crusade, at which, as the Reverend Rousseau O'Neal told the *Cincinnati Enquirer*, "There were almost no people of color in the audience."

In the sermons Graham would deliver during the mission's four evening services, he condemned racism and bigotry as sins and obstacles to a relationship with Christ. Noting their existence in various areas of the world, he specifically pointed to Cincinnati as being troubled by this plague, and stressed the importance of unity and reconciliation. During his Saturday night sermon, for example, which he delivered to an audience of mostly young people, he stated, "You may not like people of another race; you may not like people of another culture; but you can love them if you accept God in your heart."

THE DAYS BEFORE THE MISSION

Typically, on the days before and during a mission, Billy has very little free time. The opportunities he has to venture from his hotel room are usually for mission-related appointments and other scheduled activities. However, a few days before the Cincinnati Mission began, Billy found himself with some downtime. Knowing that the evening services at the stadium would be just about the only moments he would be spending outdoors, he decided to enjoy these precious moments relaxing in one of the local parks.

It was a hot afternoon, and when his car stopped at a traffic light on the way to the park, Billy encountered a group of church members, who were busy distributing cold drinks to people on the streets and in cars. Representing 360 congregations, these volunteers had joined together to distribute over 300,000 cans of soft drinks, fruit juice, and bottles of water on that hot summer day as part of one of the Cincinnati Mission's outreach programs. When one of the participants reached into the car to offer its occupants some juice, he was startled to discover that the person in the front passenger seat was none other than Billy Graham.

In earlier years, as part of his usual routine, Billy would have saturated a city. He would speak several times throughout the day, attend crusade-related events, and even hold full-court press conferences. Over the course of many decades, however, the aging evangelist had to curtail the weight of such activities, conserving his energy for the actual mission sessions. In the words of his press representative, Larry Ross, Billy Graham "is like Tiger Woods, who concentrates on the majors."

Recognizing the power of the media, however, Billy did meet with reporters on the Tuesday before the mission began. Neatly attired in a sport coat and slacks, he spoke to the assembled group, which included correspondents from Washington, D.C., Dallas-Forth Worth, and the Associated Press, as well as a large local delegation from Ohio, Indiana, and Kentucky. "My goodness!" he began, "I'm not used to facing so many cameras. I haven't given a talk or a speech in nine months, and I certainly haven't met the press." During the conference, he spoke of his basic message for the mission, stating, "I'll talk about some of the issues that face this area, but my main message is going to be Christ and what He can do in the individual life, in the family life, and in the community life. And I hope you will pray for me as well. God bless you all."

Billy also attended a reception for the board of directors of the Billy Graham Evangelistic Association (the BGEA), where he greeted old friends and briefed them on the Cincinnati venture. Graham's son Franklin represented him at a reception for state and local dignitaries, during which Ohio Governor Bob Taft stated, "We are blessed that Billy Graham has decided to return to Cincinnati for his third Mission here. And we are grateful to God for giving him strength. We hope this Mission will strengthen our resolve to unite towards reconciliation of our families and our communities."

As the week progressed, current and former team members and other mission participants arrived in the city. The sense of excitement swelled with the anticipation that the 2002 Cincinnati Mission was going to be a great success.

MONTHS OF PREPARATION

Back in his hotel room on the mission's opening day, Billy continued to read his Bible and pray. Final touches were being added to what had been a ten-month period of preparation. And although his associates were thoroughly familiar with the drill— one that was formulated in Grand Rapids, Michigan, and Charlotte, North Carolina, in 1947—they painstakingly attended to every detail of their game plan. As with all past crusades and missions, Graham's dedicated staff members considered the four days of this mission to be the centerpiece of the Billy Graham Evangelistic Association's overall program. They did not believe they served Billy Graham but a higher power, and they must not fail in their efforts.

The Graham mission has two basic goals: to seek to evangelize the community with primary emphasis on personal evangelism; and to seek to strengthen the local church for its continuing witness and discipleship through renewal and training activities during the mission's preparation period.

Every Graham mission is the result of a cooperative effort involving the evangelist, his team, local Christians and churches. Once the site and date of a mission have been confirmed, a BGEA staff member is assigned to that city to serve as mission director. The person in this position first sets up an office to serve as the mission's headquarters, and then, along with a small number of associates, begins laying the groundwork for the anticipated event. Utilizing the methods, materials, and knowledge that have been gathered during decades of experience, the director organizes local committees to assist with the extensive preparations involved. As the liaison between the Graham organization and the local community, the director is also responsible for seeing that specific policies are established in the areas of organization, finance, and follow-up in order to maintain the mission's integrity and fairness to all.

To be successful in performing the many functions involved in launching such a large-scale event, the mission director must rely on the involvement of a great number of volunteers. It has been estimated that without volunteers, thousands of professional staff members would be required to conduct a Graham mission.

The mission director works in close coordination with an executive committee, which is comprised of local clergy and laity. This committee is responsible for determining the budget of the mission, and then raising and disbursing the required funds. Its financial report, which is prepared by an independent auditing firm, is made public at the end of the mission.

In Cincinnati, the executive committee was chaired by former Bengals football star Anthony Muñoz. The officers and members of the committee represented a wide cross section of the area's spiritual and business leadership. It also reflected the racial diversity of the Christian community. The Reverend Damon Lynch, Jr., pastor of one of Cincinnati's largest African-American churches, served both as a vice chair and finance committee co-chair. Ironically, his son was active in the mission boycott movement. Before the mission began, Reverend Lynch said, "Never before in the history of our city have so many people come together, united in one common cause. Over the past year, we have built new and significant relationships as individuals, and, cooperatively, as churches."

Those who are involved with a mission—committee members and volunteers—are aware of the theological beliefs of the Graham organization, which include the standard themes of evangelical faith concerning the Bible; the Trinity; the mediating work of Christ, His resurrection, and second coming; and the need for personal salvation.

Increasingly over the years, as the outreach of his ministry has broadened, Billy, while remaining thoroughly committed to the fundamentals of evangelical doctrine, has expressed greater concern for social justice. To some of Billy's critics, his is an untenable juggling act. Those to his theological right attack him for compromising his message and insist that he stick to the old time religion of sin and salvation. Those to his theological left attack him for placing the Gospel first, at the expense of the social implications of the Christian faith.

In recent years, Graham crusades and missions have featured a new outreach program called "Love in Action: Showing God's Love in a Practical Way." It is an aspect of the Graham ministry based on Matthew 25:35: "For I was hungry and you gave me food; I was thirsty and you gave me drink; I was a stranger and you took me in." The Graham organization believes that, in addition to the preaching ministry, all missions should seize the opportunity to "put feet and hands to the Gospel." This is done through visible short-term and ongoing projects that encourage the development of caring relationships between Christians and their neighbors. The Love in Action Committee was engaged in three major programs in Cincinnati—Broad Impact, Deep Impact, and Tangible Impact.

In an effort to "provide a cup of water in God's name," those involved with the Broad Impact Program helped distribute cold drinks to over 300,000 people a few days before the start of the mission. It was the same group that had offered Billy a cold drink on his drive to the park that hot afternoon. Volunteers who participated in the Deep Impact Program worked with disadvantaged young people. They helped them with their homework, and served as mentors in after-school programs, artistic development projects, sports activities, and computer training programs. The Tangible Impact Program was a food drive, whose goal was to help provide some of the 33,000 meals that were required each week to feed the hungry of the Greater Cincinnati area. By the cut-off date of May 19th, more than 47,000 bags, containing a total of 750,000 pounds of food, had been picked up from the mission office. And during the mission itself, thousands of additional bags were distributed at the stadium following each evening's service. The outreach of the Love in Action Program is an important facet of the Graham ministry; it helps to fulfill each mission's basic purposes of bringing people to Christ and strengthening believers in their faith.

In a further effort to combine social action with evangelism during the mission experience, the Graham Team, led by Associate Evangelist Ralph Bell, conducts outreach programs in prisons, jails, and juvenile facilities within the mission's geographic area. During the Cincinnati Mission, Reverend Bell preached at over ten correctional institutions. He worked closely with chaplains, correctional officers, and volunteers to win souls and strengthen and encourage Christian inmates in their witness to their peers.

And the Graham mission is unique in that its stated objectives include making disciples—linked to the local church—of all those who come forward to accept the evangelist's invitation for personal salvation. Graham's people believe that their goals can be achieved only through the commitment of participating churches and individual Christians to pray, work, and witness in a truly cooperative manner. To this end, the Graham organization, working in coordination with the local Christian community, initiates its preparation activities at least six months prior to the mission.

In Cincinnati, specific prayer groups, involving pastors as well as lay people—men, women, and students—were organized; counselors were recruited and trained; a 3,000-voice choir was formed; ushers and security personnel were given assignments; and public relations specialists were informed of their responsibilities. In addition, and just as important, a number of committees were formed to ensure accessibility and arrangements at the stadium for those with special needs, such as children, the deaf and hard of hearing, and those who required interpreters.

And while Billy Graham and his associates may view prayer as the essential element—the *sine qua non*—of any large-scale evangelistic effort, from a practical point of view, the Friend-to-Friend program may be the most important of all the mission's undertakings. Previously called Operation Andrew, Friend-to-Friend is an effort to help ensure good turnouts at the mission services. In Cincinnati, for instance, the Paul Brown Stadium has a capacity for 63,000 people. That's a huge number of seats to fill four nights running. During the city's early planning stages of the mission, many months before the event itself, the Friend-to-Friend program went into effect. Through it, local Christians prayed for people whom they knew were in need of Christ. They cultivated friendships, and, ultimately, invited them to the mission meetings. According to the Graham organization, almost 80 percent of those who come forward at Billy's invitation are at the service because of the Friend-to-Friend program. Many months prior to the mission date, the Graham organization encourages local pastors to hold special Friend-to-Friend Sundays, encouraging church member involvement. The organization also provides brochures and videos to facilitate this effort.

As the opening day of a mission approaches, the event is advertised in local newspapers and through broadcast media, as well as on billboards, posters, and flyers. Significant pre-mission coverage helps ensure that everyone—even those outside the church's orbit—is aware that Billy Graham is coming. While the advertising campaign and media exposure help generate attendance, as do appearances by well-known musical artists, it is primarily the effectiveness of the Friend-to-Friend program that determines the number of people who show up each evening.

The sheer longevity of Graham's ministry and its decades of coverage have brought Billy Graham himself worldwide fame. His constant presence on the Gallup Poll's list of the world's ten most admired men inspires many people to attend a mission service simply because they want to see him in person. Of course, most won't be able to see him very well, especially if seated in the mid to upper reaches of a stadium. For most of those who attended the Cincinnati Mission, their best view of Billy was on one of the giant-sized screens that were mounted at each end of the field. When so viewed, Graham appeared both tanned and energetic. When seen from a closer vantage point, however, he appeared to be tired and more sedate.

Prior to one of the evening services, we met and spoke with Billy, who greeted us with warmth. It was obvious that he was clearly exhausted. We realized what a tremendous effort it must have taken for a man approaching his mid-eighties, and struggling with a variety of illnesses, to appear before tens of thousands of people on four consecutive evenings.

During these appearances, Billy's effort would be further weighted by his own sense of responsibility. He knew that among the thousands of people who would be seated in the stadium each night, there would be individuals who might never hear his message again, and whose only opportunity to receive Christ might be on those particular evenings. Furthermore, he knew that he was speaking to more than those who attended services at the stadium. Both his image and the words he would speak during this mission would be taped and used for the production of a television special, which would be seen by an even greater audience. And unlike those in attendance at the stadium, those watching him on television would see him up close and personal, and he had to look his best.

No matter how he felt physically, that night in Cincinnati, Billy knew that he had to cogently and forcefully communicate the Gospel. Observing the evangelist as he stood on the platform and spoke to the crowd, one did not have to agree with his message to recognize his act of will and courage in continuing his mission ministry.

ARRIVAL AT THE STADIUM

After meeting with Billy just a short while earlier, we took our seats in the press area, just a few hundred feet from the platform on which the evangelist would be delivering his sermon. The rain had subsided, and, although the oppressive heat and humidity had returned, the air was charged with excitement in anticipation of the program. Just prior to Billy's entering the stadium, a message flashed across the scoreboard: "Mike Williamson: call your sister at home." In the infield area, directly in front of the platform, a young man had fainted and was being tended to by two police officers. Later, we would learn of several more people who had collapsed.

Cliff Barrows began the program by leading the choir, which was seated in the end zone directly behind the platform, in "All Hail the Power of Jesus' Name." At the conclusion of this opening hymn, Billy entered the stadium. He was driven to the stage on a golf cart and escorted up the steps by two security officers. As he walked toward his seat near the podium, he greeted the guests and members of the mission's executive committee, who were already seated there. He sat down and listened intently as football greats Anthony Muñoz and Shaun Alexander offered their testimonies to the crowd before them. Then singer George Beverly Shea—Billy's old friend and associate—inspired the crowd as he sang "It Is No Secret What God Can Do." Billy appeared moved by the performance, which was met with energetic applause.

Then Billy's son Franklin walked to the podium. He spoke of the growing worldwide AIDS crisis. Franklin further described how his organizations—Samaritan's Purse and World Medical

Missions—were working to help those who suffered from this disease. He concluded his message by saying:

> There are 40 million men, women, and children infected with the HIV AIDS virus. Last year, 3 million people died as a result of AIDS. There are 5 million new cases, a figure that could eventually reach 100 million—each case representing a person with a soul made in God's image and precious to Him. They have hope in Jesus Christ. We must reach out to them, have compassion, and tell them about Christ.

Franklin paused, allowing those thoughts to sink in, and then, very simply, very directly, he introduced his father. Billy stood up and, as he had done thousands of times during the course of his ministry, moved purposefully to the podium and placed his notes on the lectern. Dressed in a dark blue suit, white shirt, and tie, he reached into his pocket, took out a pair of sunglasses, and put them on. He needed the glasses because of recent eye surgery. He would, however, take them off throughout his message, particularly when he wanted to make eye contact with the television camera that was recording his image and words for future broadcasts.

A nearly absolute silence fell over the stadium. Billy scanned the crowd, looking at the sea of expectant faces. All eyes were focused on him. His message, what he had to say, was the reason the tens of thousands of people before him had come to the stadium that evening. Billy began:

> We used to have "Youth for Christ," but now Cliff Barrows and I are going to call ourselves "Older people for Christ." Older people need Christ even more than the young people. I've known Cliff and Bev Shea for fifty years. I have never gotten angry with them, nor them with me. It's been a wonderful life together, not only in services like this, but also in prayer and in friendship.

> I don't know when we'll be back to Cincinnati; we haven't been invited yet. I do want to come back for the opening of the National Underground Railway Center.

There was a great Russian writer, Dostoyevsky, who wrote great novels, such as *Crime and Punishment* and *The Brothers Karamazov*. But there was one story he put in every novel. Do you know what it is? It is the story told in the Fifteenth Chapter of Luke. It is the story of a son who went to his father and said, "I have decided to go on my own and I'd like my inheritance; I want you to give it to me now." And the father gave him the inheritance, and the son went and had a big time.

Jesus always spoke in parables; when he gave a spiritual truth, he illustrated it with a story. Many people ask me: "What do you think God is like?" I believe the answer is in this story, more than any other place in the Bible. Literary experts call this the finest short story ever written. Here was a son who wanted all he could; he wanted to get as far away as he could. He wanted to live as he pleased and he didn't want anybody to see him. And he wasn't willing to wait for his father to die. He wanted it *now*. So he set off for a distant country; he was free to do as he pleased.

I remember we held several crusades in Hawaii, and someone was quoted in the newspaper as saying, "Everyone here is running from something, and this is the last stop. There isn't anywhere to go from here." I think people have said the same thing about Las Vegas.

Jesus said, "You serve me with your lips but your heart is far from me." Outwardly, you go to church, you've been baptized, you've been confirmed. But deep down inside, you don't really belong to Christ.

So this young man was running from himself. You have problems, you have misunderstandings, you have hurts, and you want to get away. And all around you today there are people who are doing the same. So this boy squandered everything; he had gotten it all from his father. And the Scripture says in Isaiah, "Why spend your money on something that is not real? Why work for something that doesn't really satisfy you?" Because that is what he was doing. He was doing everything for pleasure.

This story is also a picture of this young man's recognition of his need. Famine came, depression came, the stock market failed. It was probably the first time in his life that he'd ever been hungry or lacked anything material.

This physical hunger is a picture of our spiritual need. You know, there are billions of people in our world who are spiritually hungry. My son Franklin has an organization called Samaritan's Purse that does everything it can to reach the hungry people in India, and Africa, and Latin America—all over the world. And at Christmas time they send a ship full of gifts to children in various parts of the world.

This young man was not only physically hungry, he was spiritually hungry. And the Scripture says he changed himself. In other words, he began to realize how wrong he was. He began to think there was an alternative in life, that he had taken to the wrong road. Then he began to think about his father, about the servants and how they had far greater comforts and food and everything than he had where he was. And there was an alternative. There was his father's home. He did not know how he would be received, but he could go and beg his father to help him.

There is an alternative for all of you. Maybe you don't have the satisfaction and the joy and the peace you would like to have, and you've taken the wrong road somewhere. Maybe you have a wrong marriage. Whatever it is, you're on the wrong path. But there is an alternative. Jesus says there are two roads. One is broad, with all its pleasure and delights of this life, and leads to destruction. There is the narrow road, which you can take and go by the way of the cross, and it leads to heaven. It leads to eternal life. There is an alternative in Jesus Christ.

There is also the picture of a young man's repentance. The first sermon Jesus ever preached was repentance. The first sermon John the Baptist ever preached was repentance. This young man was very humble and sorry. He was now feeding the hogs; he was eating with the pigs. But this young man said to himself, I'm going to arise and go to my father. He made up a little prayer to say to his father. He said, "Father, I've sinned against heaven, and in your sight, and am no longer worthy to be called your son." He never got a chance to deliver that message. There was no trace of arrogance, he was not trying to justify what he'd done. He realized that he'd sinned, that he was on the wrong road. And he wanted to cast himself upon his father.

When King David committed the awful sin of adultery, he confessed his sin. You will find that confession in Psalm 54. God will not reject a heart that is broken and sorry for sin. That's David's prayer. God forgave him. But he had to pay a price for the sins he had committed, and his young son died.

To repent means to change, to turn around, to go in the other direction, to take another road. Will you say to God, "Lord I'm sorry, I want your forgiveness? If you will help me, I'll change the way I live." That's exactly what the young man had in mind to do. That's why we give the invitation at these meetings for you to come forward, to stand here. To step in repentance and faith. To say, "Lord, I'm here; I give myself to you." It gives people an opportunity to take a step of repentance toward God. Many of you need to take that step tonight.

And it is a picture of the young man's reconciliation. His father saw him and had compassion and ran and fell on his neck and kissed him. Do you know something? God is not waiting to condemn you or reject you. He is waiting to receive you in mercy and love. The day will come when God is going to judge the world. But today is the day of grace and salvation for all who will come and say, "Lord I am willing to change my life and put my faith in the person of Jesus, who died on the cross for my sins." Not because we deserve it, but because of what Christ has done for us through His death on the cross.

The Bible says, "The wages of sin is death, but the gift of God is eternal life." You don't have to work for it; you don't have to pay for it; He gives it to you. That means you live forever in a place called heaven.

In First Peter 2 it says, "By whose stripes we were healed." Jesus received those stripes across his back, nails in his hands, a crown of thorns on his brow. For you. If you were the only person in the world that needed Him, He would have died for you. Because there is only one way you can be justified before God and that is by the cross. Jesus died in your place.

You can only come to Christ when the Holy Spirit draws you. You can't have the attitude: "I know that I'm on the wrong road, but I'm not tired of it yet; I'll repent and come back to God somewhere down the line." That will not happen. You have to come now. You may not be able to repent then. Because the further you travel down this road away from God, the less you think you've done anything wrong. And the less you think you need to meet him. So change roads tonight.

Cincinnati may never have a moment like this in its history. What an hour this is in the history of Cincinnati and Northern Kentucky, Ohio, and Indiana.

Some of you think you are too bad for God, and that you have done too many things wrong, and have gone too far away. No. If there is any little voice inside you that says you ought to come and receive Christ as your Lord and Savior, that is the voice of the Spirit of God. If you feel a tug in your heart at all, then it is not too late. The Holy Spirit is at work, urging you to come. You come tonight. God is ready to welcome you with open arms.

That father had loved his son, no matter how far away he had gone. He sat on the front porch of his house and watched that road on which his son had left. Day after day, and month after month, and year after year. And one day, he saw a straggler coming down the road. He said, "It looks like my son." He ran to him and welcomed him, and celebrated the return of his son.

The Bible says there is joy in heaven over one person that repents. In a "Dear Abby" column years ago, I read about a teenager who was about to graduate from high school. He had a father who loved him very much and asked him what gift he would like for his graduation. He said he wanted a car. On graduation day, the father gave him a Bible, and the son slammed it down and went away. Later, the son read that his father had died. So he went home and in the house he found the Bible. When he opened it, he found a check that had been written on his graduation day for the exact amount of the cost of the car. He had missed his father's love, he had missed his car, he had missed his life entirely because of his attitude.

God is a God that loves you. He has a gift for you; He is waiting tonight to welcome you. I am going to ask you to accept the invitation by the Father, the Son, and the Holy Spirit. If you are a member of a church, if you have been baptized or confirmed but are not sure of your relationship to Christ, you come. I want hundreds of you to come. It will take a few moments. We will wait on you. You come and say, "Lord I did receive you in my heart, I did repent for my sins."

There may never be a moment like this. You come. Don't let this moment pass.

As Billy offered the invitation, people throughout the stadium began to make their way onto the infield, to the large space before the platform. Billy sat on a stool beside the podium and looked out as the choir sang the hymn "Just As I Am." At first it appeared that only a few members of the audience would come forward, but the trickle quickly became a flood. Once they had reached the infield, the inquirers were met by counselors, who provided them with printed materials and acted as their bridge to the evangelist.

Later, through Bob Paulson of *Decision* magazine, we learned of some of the people who had come forward to accept Billy's invitation. There was the man who had no intention of attending the service, but whose interest was piqued after observing the mission activities from his office window, which overlooked the Paul Brown Stadium. There was also the young married couple who came forward to accept Christ after two of their children had committed themselves during a special children's service; the young man who was met by a counselor, who amazingly turned out to be his high school football coach; and of the woman who, after having accepted Christ earlier in the week, had brought several people to the mission, six of whom made decisions.

We also learned of the woman who, while visiting Cincinnati to attend a convention, read about the mission in a newspaper advertisement and decided to come; of another young woman who attended the mission to research a school project on Billy Graham, and ended up coming forward; of the husband and wife counselors who committed themselves to full-time Christian service; of one counselor who led two of his son's former football teammates to Jesus; and of the elderly woman who, as her ailing husband gave himself to Christ, told her counselor, "This is the happiest day of my life."

We were also told of an unemployed man who had recently been released from prison, and who, through his counselor, was put in touch with a firm that just happened to be hiring people with his experience; of a young woman who learned of the mission on the local news, and ended up coming forward along with her mother, grandmother, and aunt; of a lady who happened to be passing the stadium on her way home from work, and decided to stop in just fifteen minutes before Billy delivered his message; and of the couple in their sixties who, although long active in their local church, decided to come forward that night.

That night at the Paul Brown Stadium, the choir continued to sing as Billy waited until the last people had made their way down from the grandstand. When he was satisfied that everyone who wanted to come forward had done so, he asked the inquirers to pray with him:

O God, I'm a sinner. I'm sorry for my sins. With your help, I'm willing to turn from my sin. I'm willing to change my whole way of life. Help me as I leave this place to resist temptation. May the Holy Spirit fill me. Now I am committing my life to Jesus as Lord and Savior. Amen.

The prayer ended. Billy left the platform and rode in the golf cart to a car that was waiting to take him back to the hotel. Meanwhile, counselors continued to talk with the inquirers as their quest for souls continued into the night.

AFTER THE SERVICE

Following the conclusion of the opening service, we made our way from the stadium and headed back to our hotel for a late dinner. Afterward, we returned to the stadium to observe the follow-up work that was taking place at the mission's Co-Labor station.

The Co-Labor activity—a process conceived by Charlie Riggs, director of the 1975 Jackson Crusade, and later formalized in manuals written by Tom Phillips, Riggs's assistant in Jackson—allowed for the necessary follow-up after each evening's service. It helped to ensure that local churches would soon contact the people who came forward during mission services.

As mentioned earlier, when people come forward during services to commit their lives to Christ, they are greeted by counselors. At that time, they are given cards on which they fill out some basic contact information. When the service is over, the cards are taken to the Co-Labor station, where volunteers sort and record the information.

When we walked into the Co-Labor station that evening, we found over a hundred volunteers busy at work. Most were seated in front of computers, entering information from the more than 2,500 cards that had been filled out that night. This data would also be sent to Minneapolis and added to the Graham Organization's main database. Workers in the Co-Labor station also generated letters to local pastors, informing them of the congregants from their churches who had come forward. A letter from Billy Graham would accompany these letters. As soon as the mail was metered, members of the Christian Motorcycle Association, riding with sidecars attached to their bikes, took the mail to Cincinnati's main post office.

As Billy Graham slept that night in his hotel room, the Co-Labor crew carried on its work until after 3:00 AM, pausing only occasionally for a cup of coffee or a sandwich. When he awoke in the morning, Billy would find a sheet under his door, listing the number of people who had come forward that evening.

MAINTAINING THE CHALLENGE

One can safely conclude that it isn't easy being Billy Graham. Aside from the pressures inherent in maintaining his ministry, he is also responsible for keeping the Billy Graham Evangelistic Association, which has been built on his name and reputation, on an even keel.

Thus, his mission in Cincinnati, following a nine-month hiatus from public appearances, was a crucial affirmation of his continuing presence on the national scene. The enthusiastic response he received from this mission's audiences, as well as the favorable coverage he garnered in the media, proved that people continue to expect and welcome his public ministry. He demonstrated in Cincinnati that he was still capable of holding a successful, major meeting, and doing so on a large scale. On the closing evening of the mission, the attendance record of the Paul Brown Stadium was broken. The success of this mission energized and humbled Billy, who has always been steadfast and strong when facing the constant challenges to him and to his ministry.

As Billy prepared to leave Cincinnati, he realized that the true impact of this mission may not be known for many years to come. What he did know, however, was that it brought together 20,000 volunteers from 964 churches, representing 67 denominations. He also knew that during this mission, he preached to 201,600 people, and 8,497 of them responded to his invitation to receive, or recommit, to Christ.

As Billy Graham returned to his home in Montreat, North Carolina, members of his staff would be working at full speed to organize his next mission, which would be taking place in another four months in Dallas, Texas.

Billy beckons those in attendance to come forward and dedicate their lives to Christ.

2

Beginnings

BILLY GRAHAM'S LIFE BEGAN ON A dairy farm in Charlotte, North
Carolina, on November 7, 1918. The first child of Morrow and
Frank Graham, he was named William Franklin Graham, Jr.
Although the Grahams were doctrinally strict Scottish Presbyte-
rians, they tended toward moderation in rearing Billy, who, as a
young boy, and contrary to his mother's wishes and prayers,
aspired to become a baseball player rather than a minister.

Billy's early years were those of a typical farm boy. Responsible for pulling his weight on the farm, he was assigned such
chores as milking the cows in the early morning and filling the
feed troughs after school. Billy was influenced at that time not
only by his parents and his environment, but also by former
Army sergeant Reese Brown, the farm's African-American fore-
man. It was Brown who helped Billy learn to drive the family's
GMC truck. Years later, when looking back at his youth, Billy
would say that Brown was "one of the strongest men I ever saw.
He had a tremendous capacity for work and great intelligence. He
had a profound effect on my life in its earliest years."

At the age of sixteen, Billy underwent a religious crisis not
uncommon to youngsters living in an atmosphere permeated by
the trappings of the old-time religion. His parents were godly
Christians, but Billy had yet to make a personal commitment to
Christ. His moment of truth occurred when Mordechai Ham, an
evangelist whose preaching of the Gospel was often accompanied
by racist and anti-Semitic remarks, was invited by a group of
local businessmen to visit Charlotte for a series of tent meetings.

After attending several of those meetings, Billy gave his heart to Christ. Among others who were moved and motivated by Ham's preaching were brothers Grady and T.W. Wilson. Both would become Billy Graham's lifelong friends and key associates in his ministry.

The three young men enrolled at Bob Jones College (now Bob Jones University) in Cleveland, Tennessee, where the fiery evangelist of the 1920s had retired to develop a training school for Christian workers. Finding Jones's very narrow educational philosophy and the school's restrictive social code too harsh, Billy left after one year, continuing his studies at the Florida Bible Institute (now Trinity College) in Tampa. It was there that Billy made his decision to enter the ministry and where he first demonstrated his God-given talent for preaching—a gift that was destined to take him across the nation and throughout the world.

After graduating from the Institute, Billy sensed a need for further training, particularly in secular subjects. He enrolled at Wheaton College in Illinois. At that time, it was the most respected evangelical college in the United States. It was at Wheaton that he would study anthropology—a mind-expanding subject for one who had been brought up in the pre-civil rights revolution South, where blacks were regarded as racially inferior.

While studying at Wheaton, Billy supported himself by hauling furniture and pastoring at a local church. And it was while attending this school that he met his life's partner, Ruth Bell, whom he married in 1943. The daughter of medical missionary Dr. L. Nelson Bell, Ruth was born and raised in China. Her father would come to play an increasingly important role in Billy's career. A lifelong Presbyterian, Dr. Bell—as his son-in-law always referred to him—was instrumental in broadening Billy's awareness and appreciation of the status of Christian faith within the major denominations. Eventually, this understanding would enable Billy to include Christians from many denominations as sponsors of his citywide crusades.

After graduating from Wheaton in 1943, Billy became pastor of the Village Baptist Church in nearby Western Springs. Early in his pastorate, he received an offer from Torrey Johnson, a well-known Chicago minister, who aired a weekly religious radio program called *Songs in the Night*. Johnson asked Graham to take over the broadcast, which aired on Sunday evenings and was heard in many eastern states. The program had become an overwhelming task to Johnson, who was busy developing plans for an organization called Youth for Christ. Billy was able to convince his skeptical church leadership to underwrite the radio program, and within a matter of weeks—with the help of the popular singer George Beverly "Bev" Shea—*Songs in the Night* became self-sustaining.

Soon Johnson was after Billy again. This time, he sought the young pastor's help in the building of Youth for Christ. And on May 20, 1944, with nearly 3,000 servicemen and young people crowding Chicago's Orchestra Hall, Billy, who claimed to have experienced "the worst fit of stage fright" in his life, gave the sermon. Responding to Billy's invitation to commit their lives to Christ, forty-two attendees came forward on that memorable occasion. It was enough to convince Johnson that the young evangelist was the right man to expand this new organization into a national movement.

When Johnson asked Billy to resign his pastorate and travel the country as a field representative for Youth for Christ, Billy agreed to do so. It would prove to be a watershed decision in the former Carolina farm boy's life. Over the next several years, Billy's work with Youth for Christ would take him to many cities in the United States and abroad. Through it, he would meet many of the people who would become the nucleus of his own evangelistic organization.

While Billy had achieved significant success in his Youth for Christ activities, he was determined to conduct full-scale citywide campaigns. He held the first of these meetings in 1947 in his hometown of Charlotte, North Carolina. By 1948, Billy had organized a team of coworkers that would hold evangelistic rallies in cities with larger populations. That year, he also accepted the presidency of Northwestern Schools, a Bible college in Minneapolis that had been founded by William B. Riley. Billy first met

Riley, who was a fundamentalist from the Midwest, during his days at the Florida Bible Institute. At age twenty-nine, Billy was the youngest college president in the nation; and he stayed at Northwestern until 1952. During the time he served there, Billy turned over the administrative duties of his own organization into the capable hands of his close friend George Wilson, who would eventually become the business genius behind the Graham organization's success.

> **Q.** Other than your parents, Ruth, and your immediate family, who has made the greatest impact on your life?
>
> **A.** *When I married Ruth, I didn't dream that to come with her was one of the most remarkable men I have ever known, a man who has had tremendous influence on my life. That was Dr. Nelson Bell, her father. He was moderator of the Presbyterian Church in his last year. He was seventy-nine, and died that year he was moderator. He was a great churchman and he was a great doctor.*

In September of 1949, Billy, together with his team of old friends and associates, including Grady Wilson, song leader Cliff Barrows, and soloist Bev Shea, began what they had planned as a three-week-long series of meetings. The meetings were held in a tent that had been erected at the corner of Washington and Hill Streets in Los Angeles. Just prior to those meetings, which would prove to be the most important of his career, Billy had endured a dark night of the soul, during which his faith in the inspiration and authority of the Scriptures was severely tested. After a period of study, prayer, and conversations with Henrietta Mears, director of religious education at the First Presbyterian Church of Hollywood, Billy overcame the problem. He prayed, "Father, I am going to accept this as Thy Word—by faith. I will believe this to be Your inspired Word." As Billy would later write in his autobiography, "In my heart and mind, I knew a spiritual battle in my soul had been fought and won."

During the course of the Los Angeles meetings, there was a series of sensational conversions, including those of a famous cowboy singer, a former Olympic athlete, and a wiretapper who worked for a crime syndicate. This brought Graham and his team widespread media attention, and what was initially planned as a three-week campaign, lasted for several more.

The most important media response to the Los Angeles meetings came from newspaper magnate William Randolph Hearst, who sent a message to his editors across the country, ordering them to "puff Graham." In the wake of the positive publicity generated by Hearst's message, invitations began to pour in from major cities across the country, asking the Graham organization to hold campaigns. And Graham's ministry was on its way.

Next, in 1950, the Graham team took its campaign to Boston to honor a commitment Billy had made a few years earlier to Harold John Okengea. Minister of the historic Park Street Church, Okengea had been (and would continue to be) a close adviser to Billy. In Boston, the young evangelist repeated his Los Angeles triumph, climaxing his campaign by preaching to an audience of 16,000 at the Boston Garden.

The popularity of Graham and his organization continued to grow. During the next series of meetings, which took place in Columbia, South Carolina, the state's governor joined Billy on the platform one evening. Billy also had a late-night meeting with Henry Luce, publisher of *Time Magazine*. Luce, who had heard Graham preach in Columbia's Township Auditorium, decided to support him by running articles about his work.

While he was in Columbia, Billy recruited Wills Haymaker to his staff. A former aide to the evangelists Gypsy Smith and Bob Jones, Haymaker would come up with the term "crusade" to define Billy's increasingly successful meetings. Sensing the implications of a nationwide movement toward individual salvation, Billy would soon employ Haymaker's term and speak of a "crusade to bring America to her knees in repentance of sin and faith toward God."

By 1950, Billy had become so well established as a national

personality that he was invited to the White House to meet President Harry Truman in July of that year. Their encounter was the first of many that Billy would have with the nation's commanders in chief. Later that year, Billy took steps to solidify his status as the nation's foremost evangelical leader. On November 5, he launched the *Hour of Decision*—a thirty-minute, weekly nationwide radio broadcast featuring hymns, a reading from the Scriptures, and a message from Billy. By the end of the month, donations from listeners flowed steadily into his Minneapolis headquarters. Billy quickly signed documents, establishing the Billy Graham Evangelistic Association. A nonprofit organization, the BGEA would come to be known for its spiritual resolve and financial integrity.

During the early 1950s, America was preoccupied with the Korean War, as well as McCarthyism on the home front. Billy, who abhorred the Wisconsin senator's tactics, but articulated the same strong anti-communist position in his preaching, held crusades in several major cities, including Dallas-Fort Worth, Detroit, Seattle, and Washington, DC.

In 1954, Billy and his associates journeyed to Britain for their most challenging endeavor—a twelve-week-long crusade in London. The city was the capital of a nation with a national church, albeit one practically devoid of worshippers. Struggling against apathy, a hostile press, and damp weather, Billy preached at Harrington Arena, a 12,000-seat indoor stadium in north London. On the closing day of the crusade, Graham spoke at White City Stadium and Wembley Stadium. Despite a heavy rainstorm, an audience of 120,000 gathered at Wembley to hear the words of the evangelist. At that time, it was the largest crowd in the history of the United Kingdom to assemble for a religious event. Of the more than 2 million people who attended the London Crusade, 38,000 came forward to make decisions for Christ.

While he was in London, Billy had the opportunity to meet with Prime Minister Winston Churchill. During their conversation, the statesman questioned Billy in particular about the Second Coming of Christ. Afterward, when he spoke of their meeting, Billy remarked, "I felt like I had shaken the hand of Mr. History."

By decade's end, Billy would make history himself, as he continued preaching to growing audiences throughout the United States, Europe, and Asia. He conducted a memorable sixteen-week crusade that was held in New York City's Madison Square Garden in 1957, and a four-month tour of Australia in 1959, during which he addressed audiences totaling more than 3 million.

During the 1960s, Billy and his team journeyed to Africa and the Middle East. He also returned to London, New York, Australia, and Los Angeles, where he addressed the largest crowd in the history of that city's famed Coliseum. During that decade, Billy also strengthened his ties with the American Roman Catholic and Jewish communities. In 1968, during the Pittsburgh Crusade, Bishop John Wright would call upon the faithful of his Pittsburgh diocese to pray for the success of the crusade saying, "Even those who do not share in other elements of the Crusade theology rejoice that a powerful voice will be lifted in Pittsburgh to proclaim the divinity of our Saviour Jesus Christ."

Billy's relationship with the Jewish community would also continue to grow following the release in 1971 of *His Land*, an hour-long film produced by the BGEA's World Wide Pictures subsidiary. In it, the evangelist forcefully articulates his theological understanding of the State of Israel. Screened in churches throughout the United States and Canada, *His Land* has been hailed by Jewish leaders as perhaps the finest Christian statement on Israel since the state's founding in 1948.

Billy's sympathetic views of Israel and his concern for the plight of Soviet Jews prompted Roy Larson, religion editor of the *Chicago Sun Times*, to comment, "Sizeable segments of the evangelical movement have long been afflicted with anti-Semitism; Graham's efforts to eradicate this illness have brought him much deserved praise from the nation's Jewish community."

In the 1970s, Billy continued his major domestic and international city crusades; but a growing emphasis on his television ministry enabled his crusades to take place in smaller cities than they had in the past. They were held in mid-sized localities, in places such as Albuquerque, New Mexico; Lubbock, Texas; and

Jackson, Mississippi. Although the live audiences to which he spoke were smaller than those in the major cities, his sermons were taped and presented to television audiences everywhere. These smaller locations became virtual television studios. The expansion of his television ministry also made it possible for Billy to cut down on the actual number of days he spent in a crusade city. For example, his first crusade in Jackson, Mississippi, in 1952 lasted four weeks; the 1975 crusade lasted ten days.

Billy also held a number of breakthrough meetings in the 1970s with trips to then-Soviet bloc nations Poland and Hungary, and a crusade on the campus of Notre Dame University in South Bend, Indiana—an evangelical "first." During the following decade, Graham held pioneering meetings in East Germany and Czechoslovakia, and penetrated the heart of the communist world by preaching in the Soviet Union and the People's Republic of China. In the 1990s, Billy traveled to North Korea and held crusades in Argentina, West Germany, and Hong Kong.

From the mid-1970s through 2002, Billy conducted crusades or missions (as his meetings have been called since Fresno, California in 2001) in more than seventy U.S. cities. His schedule for 2003 includes missions in San Diego and Oklahoma City.

Graham's interest in promoting world evangelism led the BGEA to hold three meetings in Amsterdam between 1983 and 2000 to assist Christian workers—particularly those from the Third World—in their proclamation of the Gospel. Closer to home, the Graham organization established the Billy Graham Training Center, a facility located near Ashville, North Carolina, where "the laity can study the Bible in depth and be trained to reach the lost for Christ, thereby serving more effectively within the local church."

At Montreat, Billy and Ruth enjoy regular visits from their five children—all of whom are happily married and enjoy productive lives—and their many grandchildren and great-grandchildren. Their daughter Gigi has written several books and is active in her local church; Ann, a Bible teacher and author, has addressed conferences and church groups throughout the world; Bunny (Ruth), a former acquisitions editor at a major publishing house, is the author of a Bible storybook for children; Franklin, in addition to directing the day-to-day activities of the BGEA, heads the Christian relief organizations Samaritan's Purse and World Medical Missions; and Ned, an ordained minister, is the president of East Gate Ministries International, an organization whose ministry includes the distribution of Bibles in the People's Republic of China.

Advancing age and infirmities have led Billy to curtail his once arduous schedule. Today, he spends most of his time at home in Montreat, where he and Ruth will soon observe their sixtieth wedding anniversary. Billy still rises for prayer and Bible study, and devotes a portion of his time to overseeing the activities of the BGEA.

Billy and Ruth Graham at home in Montreat, North Carolina. [c.1975]

3

A Day at Home

MONTREAT IS SO TINY THAT IT DOES not appear on most road maps of North Carolina. Although it is the home of Montreat-Anderson College and the Montreat Conference Center of the Presbyterian Church, first-time visitors usually need detailed directions to find either place. Every year, thousands of people drive through the small village of Black Mountain, make a left turn off its main street, and continue about a mile and a half down a tree-lined road on their way to the conference center. Guests there attend retreats and meetings, study, swim, and enjoy other modes of relaxation amid the visual beauty of the Blue Ridge Mountains. Most people don't even realize that during the short ride from Black Mountain to the conference grounds, they have driven past the office of Billy Graham. And they may be even more surprised to learn that they have also passed about a thousand feet below the mountain home of the world-renowned evangelist.

There are, of course, many people who know that Billy lives in Montreat. Some travel great distances with the hope of meeting him personally. During much of his career, however, Billy has been more commonly associated with Minneapolis, the location of his organization's headquarters, than with the mountains of western North Carolina.

It was on a bright Monday morning in the spring of 1975 that I drove through this picturesque hamlet. The azaleas were beginning to blossom and the air was filled with a fragrant freshness. I had flown into the Charlotte airport from New York the night before, and was on my way to meet with Billy Graham. I had known Billy since 1969, when I served on the national staff of the American Jewish Committee. From that year until 1974, I kept in touch with him by mail and telephone. On several occasions, I met him in New York and in other cities where his crusades were being held. In 1975, a year after I left the committee, I wrote to Billy, asking if I could do a book on a day in his life. He very graciously agreed, which was the reason I found myself driving through the beautiful Carolina countryside that morning.

For many reasons, this remote part of the United States was a logical spot for Billy and Ruth to make their home. Montreat provided a serene oasis and quiet shelter where Billy has always been able to rest, study, and prepare for his incredibly complex and demanding public schedule. For much of his ministry, the evangelist spent an average of nine to ten months a year traveling throughout the world. Montreat was also the place where Ruth's parents, Dr. and Mrs. L. Nelson Bell, made their home upon returning from missionary service in China. It was only natural that when Billy became a full-time evangelist and began to spend most of his time away from home, Ruth would want to settle close to her family.

The Grahams' first home was a small cottage located near the bottom of the mountain. It was there that three of the five Graham children were born. Later, Billy and Ruth decided to build a modest home on top of the slope. Although the evangelist has been entertained in presidential residences, imperial palaces, sumptuous mansions, and some of the world's poshest hotels, he is happiest when in his simple but spacious log house. There he is surrounded by family, his closest friends and associates, and the spectacular grandeur of the Blue Ridge Mountains.

As I continued my drive, I looked forward to seeing Billy and visiting with him in the comfortable atmosphere of his home. When I reached Black Mountain, I realized that I was a half hour early for my appointment, so I walked through the two-block center of town, where I bought a copy of the local newspaper. As far as I could determine, no one in the village seemed preoccupied with the fact that a world-famous personality lived less than two miles away; that a man who consistently appeared in the top ranks of America's most admired personalities was their neighbor. Not that I had expected to find kids hawking maps that pointed to the Graham house, the way they direct tourists to stars' homes in Hollywood; nor had I imagined seeing shop windows with Billy Graham T-shirts or autographed photos on display. But I *had* expected, at the very least, to see a signpost or some other small indication that this place was just minutes from the home of Billy Graham.

The folks who lived in the area were more concerned with the price of agricultural commodities than whether Billy was at home or on one of his lengthy trips. They treated Billy and Ruth with respect, just as they did with the region's banker, newspaper editor, and other residents.

At precisely ten o'clock, I drove under the Montreat arch, turned left, and then made another left into the driveway of the modern colonial building that housed Graham's executive office. There I was greeted by Stephanie Wills, the evangelist's personal secretary, who directed me to the office of T.W. Wilson, Billy's childhood friend and closest aide.

One of T.W.'s major responsibilities was to serve as a buffer between Graham and the enormous number of people who wanted to reach him. He was a large man, whose often-serious face was highlighted by eyes that seemed to ask, "Who are you? And why are you making demands on Billy's already impossible schedule?" Obviously, Billy had to severely limit the amount of time he was able to give any individual or group. T.W. was also Billy's traveling companion. Along with his brother, Grady, T.W. was the person Billy was most able to relax with when on the road.

Although relatively few people outside the Graham organization knew of him, T.W. was a forceful and convincing preacher in his own right. However, in serving Billy and the organization, T.W. remained outside the constant public glare that surrounded the evangelist. There was little doubt that he filled his role as a faithful and competent aide with true equanimity, and not without great sacrifice to his personal life and family. As was the case with many of Billy's long-time associates, T.W. could have formed his own organization and gained wide recognition in the evangelical community. Instead, this very gracious and genial man, who inspired trust and respect, remained at Billy's side. His inner stability and strong fiber characterized the integrity of many of Graham's people.

T.W. was aware of why I had traveled to Montreat on that beautiful day. As he came out of his office, there was a twinkle in his eye and broad smile on his face, and he greeted me with old-fashioned southern warmth and hospitality. After inquiring about my trip, T.W. offered to take me on a tour of the facility. I saw the library where Billy kept his research materials, the projection room where he viewed the rushes from his World Wide Pictures subsidiary, and the storage room where mementos from decades of world recognition had been carefully catalogued and preserved. T.W. also took me upstairs to the spacious, comfortable meeting room, which was designed to accommodate very large groups.

As we toured the building, I realized that this was my first real glimpse into the world of Billy Graham—a world that few people had ever seen—and it slowly began to dawn on me that the life of this spiritual leader was far more complex and difficult than I had ever imagined. What I had just witnessed was only the beginning; there would be much more that I would come to learn.

We soon found ourselves back in T.W.'s office, where I took a seat and waited for my meeting. I thought about Billy and wondered what made him tick. What was in his psyche and character that enabled him to assume such a strenuous ministry? And what resources were available to help him sustain his exhausting lifestyle? I knew that I would probably never be able to fully answer these questions, but I was determined to learn something more about Billy Graham, the person. My thoughts were suddenly interrupted by the sound of T.W.'s voice. He was on the telephone with someone at Billy's house and was told that Billy, who had been working on some correspondence with Stephanie Wills, was now ready to receive me.

We left the office and climbed into a late-model station

wagon. Wilson got behind the wheel and drove from the parking area, turning onto a narrow road that circled up the mountain. The view was lovely, even though we seemed to be perched on the side of a steep cliff for most of the drive. In a few minutes, we came to a large gate that blocked the road. T.W., who had been in radio contact with the Graham house, touched a switch that was attached to the car's sun visor and the gate opened electronically. I appreciated this need for security in such an isolated area of the mountain.

The road continued to curve upward for a short distance before we arrived at a clearing that ended abruptly at the mouth of a small driveway. Two cars were parked in front of the house; one was Billy's, the other Ruth's. As we got out of the station wagon, I heard loud barking and turned to see two large German shepherds running and jumping behind a fence. T.W. took my arm and led me to the entrance of the house. I looked up and was most pleasantly surprised to see Billy Graham waiting in the doorway.

A WARM GREETING

As I neared the evangelist, I couldn't help but notice his striking physical appearance. He was tall and slim with a mane of blonde-gray hair, a long and deeply tanned face, perfect white teeth, and blue eyes. And when he smiled, his face took on a bright glow. To me, it seemed likely that at least part of his success was due to the face with which he had been blessed. He was in his fifties at the time of my visit, and he looked healthy, alert, and quite hand-some. It was as if his physical attraction was meant to compli-ment his charismatic personality, his agile mind, and his tremendous powers of communication. In addition, he had an inexplicable innocence about him, an aura of honesty. People immediately sensed his sincerity and knew he was a genuine per-son, not a fabricated, well-packaged product that had been pro-grammed to please and charm.

Graham shook my hand warmly and led me into the house.

We hadn't seen each other for some time, and he asked how I had been. We passed through a hallway filled with paintings, photographs, and memorabilia before entering a very large, comfortable room that was dominated by a huge fireplace. As Billy and I took seats on facing couches, T.W. excused himself and returned to the office.

I felt the need to remind Billy why I was there, but he quickly assured me that he understood my purpose in coming, and that he would do everything he could to make my visit worthwhile. I told him to feel free to ask me to leave the room if he needed to discuss confidential matters either on the telephone or with visiting staff. Laughing, he said that there was very little, if anything, he wouldn't want me to hear. I was immediately struck by the innate generosity he extended in allowing me to observe him. He had a true gift of being able to make a person feel at ease, and as he spoke, I began to relax. I believed that my presence was not going to be too much of an intrusion. I would also come to realize that Billy Graham was very much in command of himself, and that no one, no matter how fine his motivation or noble his purpose, could inhibit him from pursuing his own agenda.

A BUSY DAY AHEAD

When we began our discussion, Billy gave me a brief outline of the day's schedule. It happened to be an especially busy time for the evangelist. He planned to catch up on a backlog of correspondence, including phone calls and letters; he also needed to go over his newspaper columns, and tape two messages for the *Hour of Decision* radio show; plus he wanted to work on the second draft of a book he was writing on angels. He also had an appointment with BGEA public relations director Don Bailey, who was coming from Atlanta to discuss media coverage for the Jackson Crusade. And finally, because he would be leaving Montreat in a couple days and be gone for two weeks, Billy wanted to spend some time with Ruth.

As Billy described his impossible-sounding schedule, the

telephone rang. It was T.W., calling to say that a reporter for *The Washington Post* was on the phone and wanted to talk to Billy about the deteriorating situation in Southeast Asia. Billy asked T.W. to have the reporter call back the next day. The call gave me the opportunity to inquire about the manner in which Graham communicated with the media. Obviously, if Billy had something to say on any issue, he simply called the wire services with a statement, and his comment would be transmitted immediately throughout the nation and the world. More often, though, the media sought Graham's opinion on public issues, and they would write, call, wire, or sometimes just show up at the Montreat office, looking for a story.

Since almost anything he said was newsworthy, Graham learned a long time ago that he had to be circumspect in his handling of the press. And while he sincerely wanted to cooperate with the media, and realized that reporters were always in need of fresh information, he also had to bear in mind that whenever he spoke on the record, he was, in effect, representing tens of millions of evangelicals who highly valued his views on the major issues. Furthermore, Graham always had to remember that his basic constituency, while holding theological views similar to his own, was far from monolithic on public matters, as well as many moral and ethical questions. So he could never be too far ahead or behind his many followers when articulating his own positions.

The fact is that over the years, Graham has been consistently ahead of the evangelical community on such major diverse issues as race relations, ecumenism, war, and the evangelical lifestyle. He has brought evangelicals, particularly those in the United States, into a much broader social and political context than many would have thought possible twenty-five years earlier. However, Graham has always been careful not to crusade or take on the self-righteous tone of the do-gooder. His views are consistently formulated on Biblical grounds, adding to the strength of his opinions. Thus, he has been able to communicate to evangelicals a scriptural *raison d'être* for social concern and action. It should also be said that although Graham articulates his views forcefully, intelligently, and, at times, courageously, he does so with grace and a total absence of guile or self-serving posturing.

Graham also realized that there were some people in the media who distorted his comments, and others who wanted nothing better than to catch him in inconsistencies. Some yearned to identify him with unethical behavior or personal scandal. But anyone harboring such wishes has always been frustrated and disappointed. In a world pervaded by greed, envy, and corruption, Graham, who has been subjected to intense personal and professional scrutiny, has proven himself and his organization to be forthright and beyond reproach.

Indeed, one of the stones at the foundation of Graham's ministry has been the unshakeable belief that in order to fulfill his mission, he must conduct his activities with the highest ethical standards. Even as I sat with him on that day, decades after the formation of the original Graham Team, Billy clearly recalled the day in Modesto, California, when he had asked each of his associates to write down what they understood to be the classic public criticism of evangelists and mass evangelism.

The first and most important item on that list concerned finances. In order to dispel any notion or possibility of financial wrongdoing or mismanagement, Graham, as early as 1950—at the urging of the late Dr. Jesse Bader of the National Council of Churches—established the nonprofit Billy Graham Evangelistic Association. The BGEA would become the channel through which the ever-increasing income from his ministry would flow. In addition, Graham decided that he would no longer accept the "love offering" traditionally given to evangelists at the conclusion of a series of meetings. Instead, he and his associates received salaries. And while Billy earned a very comfortable living, it was hardly commensurate with the income of most corporate executives of major companies. Graham also received income from book royalties, as well as fees for articles and his newspaper column; however, these funds were held in trust for the benefit of his family. Even gifts from heads of state and other luminaries, ranging from golf clubs to stereos to silver tea services, which T.W. had shown me earlier in the office storage room, were not used by the Grahams. All of this has, of course, been reported in the media. Yet there are writers who periodically investigated Graham's finances in the hope of discovering irregularities.

Although he has a highly competent public relations staff, Billy normally deals directly with the media. His people set up interviews, particularly in crusade cities or places where he has long-standing speaking dates, but reporters who are experienced in dealing with the Graham organization usually try to reach him through a close personal aide. *The Washington Post* correspondent evidently fit into this category, and I wondered what Billy would say to him when they spoke.

GRAHAM'S "ECUMENICITY"

Billy Graham is not ecumenical in the same sense that the National or World Council of Churches is. In good conscience, he cannot include certain Christians in his work, nor can he exclude them from his call of personal redemption and individual commitment to Christ. He is, however, ecumenical in the sense that he will not accept an invitation to hold a citywide crusade or mission unless the majority of churches and pastors in the locality desire his presence.

Unlike major evangelists who came before him, and quite different from dyed-in-the-wool contemporary fundamentalists, Graham can and does make common cause with ministers and members of mainline denominational churches. His main criterion for cooperation has always been that crusades are aimed at achieving personal salvation through Christ. Thus, Graham's "ecumenicity" is a constant source of discussion and dissention among the ranks of American evangelicals. Divisive personalities, such as John R. Rice, Bob Jones, Jr., and Carl McIntire, have used the issue of Graham's "cooperative evangelism" to attack Billy, both professionally and personally. Indeed, some of Graham's most vitriolic critics are not found among secularists or liberal churchmen but within the ranks of certain segments of the evangelical fundamentalist camp. At times, the scorn heaped upon Graham by these believers extended far beyond both the bounds of common decency and the uncommon grace many of his critics claim to have achieved through faith in Christ.

It should also be said that Graham's ecumenical spirit has confused many grass-roots Christians, who have trouble relating to new trends and currents. The situation of a college friend comes to mind; he had taken a pastorate in Wisconsin and almost lost his pulpit when, in the first sermon he ever preached, he praised Graham's ministry. Confusion over Graham's activities sometimes caused normally intelligent people to act in a ludicrous fashion, as was the case in 1965, when the women's society of a New England-based Baptist church held a prayer meeting to decide whether to pray for the success of the Boston Crusade.

In spite of the criticism, there is little doubt that Graham's recognition of the possibility of evangelical faith within the main bodies of Christian churches has broadened both his ministry and its potential outreach. And in a real sense, he, more than any person in twentieth-century America, has established evangelical Christianity as the mainstream religion in the United States.

Like Jonathan Edwards, Charles Finney, and Dwight Lyman Moody, whose contributions influenced the growth of American evangelism, Billy Graham has made a great impact upon the whole fabric of modern American life. His influence has been deep-seated and far-reaching. And although his ministry has been conducted in some of the most turbulent and tension-filled decades of American history, he has never compromised his message. And an uncertain society has always seemed to welcome the positive, salvation-oriented course of Graham's preaching—a lesson the liberal church leadership has, apparently, not yet learned. The timeless quality of his message provides answers in a world where, at times, there seem to be only questions.

Graham recognizes the reality of difficult social and moral problems, but also believes such issues can be resolved by resorting to scriptural patterns within the overall framework of the redemptive work of Christ. He provides that which the liberal churches do not: a foundation of eternal life and credibility upon which one may make and execute plans for the reversal of wrongs and the development of a better world order.

The liberal churchman who rushed to Birmingham, or Selma, Alabama, did so out of genuine compassion and a large measure of guilt for the churches' role in the oppression of blacks in America. That gesture, however, has not been enough to resolve the basic human questions implicit in racial tension. Very often, the liberal white Christian has been all for settling matters in the Deep South, but has resisted changing the status quo in his northern suburban neighborhood.

In his approach to racial issues, Graham points to the need for changed hearts, which he believes can come only through acceptance of Christ. And he offers what he believes to be eternally valid guidelines for meeting individual needs, helping the body as well as the soul, feeding and nourishing the whole person. In talking over the years with a number of black pastors, I was convinced that Graham's approach had much potential for achieving racial unity. And while attending the Jackson Crusade, I would witness firsthand the efficacy of his long-standing effort in this area.

In evaluating Graham's motivations in the area of social justice, one must bear in mind that, by his own definition, he is first and foremost an "evangelist." In a statement issued in 1973, he said:

> I am convinced that God called me to be a New Testament evangelist, not an Old Testament prophet! While some may interpret an evangelist to be primarily a social reformer or a political activist, I don't! An evangelist is a proclaimer of the message of God's love and grace in Jesus Christ, and the necessity of repentance and faith.

Graham has long been the unofficial leader of the world's millions of evangelical Christians. Given his fame, global outreach, and uncommon gift for communication, it really could not have been otherwise. Yet he very gladly shares a leadership position with other well-known and competent evangelicals, and is careful to work within existing structures. Billy Graham is not an empire builder. Rather, he has used his influence to bring several evangelical factions together for common, positive purposes. He was the driving force behind the 1966 Berlin Congress on Evangelism; his concern for more widespread evangelical discussions of urgent social concerns brought the nation's evangelicals together in 1968; and his suggestions on the need for dialogue between Western and third-world Christians gave birth to the 1974 Lausanne Conference.

His irenic approach has done much to clarify evangelical strategy, as well as inspire better interpersonal relations between believers. This last point is no small matter when one considers that many evangelicals spend an inordinate amount of time analyzing and criticizing the faith perspectives of other believers. And while there have been some evangelicals in the past who talked about joining forces to evangelize the world, their goals often failed to come together.

Graham has achieved considerable success as a motivator and facilitator, a catalyst willing to put his prestige on the line for the sake of cooperation and unity.

ABOUT RUTH GRAHAM

The morning seemed to fly by and at 12:15, Graham, who had been up since 6:00, was ready for lunch. He went into the kitchen and came back with a tray of cheese, tomato, and lettuce sandwiches; apples; a pitcher of iced tea; and a pot of hot coffee. Ruth had fixed the lunch before leaving for a meeting of the ladies society of the Presbyterian Church. It was the first social function she attended in four months. Ruth had been recuperating from a serious fall she had taken at her daughter's home in Milwaukee. She had undergone extensive treatment for head and leg injuries, and Billy was very concerned about her condition. However, he also told me that she was on her way to a complete recovery, which was confirmed by her ability to drive down the mountain that morning.

I looked forward to meeting Ruth Graham later that day. Widely respected throughout the evangelical world, she was well known for her intelligence and sophistication. During her years at as a student at Wheaton College, Ruth was described by her housemother as someone who possessed "the most beautiful Christian character of any young person I have ever known." The Grahams remained close to Wheaton. Ruth received an honorary doctorate degree there, and Billy regarded the late V. Raymond Edman, the school's long-time president, as a valued adviser.

> **Q.** What are your favorite forms of recreation?
>
> **A.** *I try to go swimming every day if I can get to a pool in a hotel, motel, or something like that. I try to walk every day at least one hour and do some calisthenics. I was a jogger for years, and then I played golf every single day except Sunday for years, all over the world.*

Harold Lindsell, a good friend of Billy's and scholarly editor of *Christianity Today*, who knew and dated Ruth before she met her future husband said, "Fifty percent of what Billy is, is due to his wife, Ruth. She is a strong person in his life, a confidante, a critic of a constructive nature, a wise counselor." Other friends of the Grahams have told me of Ruth's strong influence on her husband in the areas of literature and art. She has suggested many of the books Billy reads. In addition, Ruth, along with her father, Dr. Bell, demonstrated to Billy the existence of faith within the major denominations. This crucial lesson for Graham enabled him to broaden the scope of his ministry. It was quite a change from the narrowly interpreted Christian faith he had studied at Bob Jones University and the Florida Bible Institute. There, Graham had been taught to be wary of mainline denominational life, which was believed to be rife with liberalism and, therefore, open to the compromise of the Gospel in order to achieve social goals.

Fortunately, the dynamic, informed, and deeply held faith of Dr. Bell, a dedicated and lifelong member of the Presbyterian Church, would influence and expand Billy's beliefs. Closer at hand, Graham was influenced by Ruth, a strong Christian woman who was a Presbyterian to his Southern Baptist—providing a degree of ecumenicity in their household.

A SHARE IN THE CALLING

By 1:00, we had polished off the remains of our lunch. Food apparently held no great attraction for Billy, who told me that because he ate out so much, he preferred very simple meals at home. On the road, he often ordered food and had it brought to his room. I found it amazing that he looked so good after eating hotel food for so many years.

Graham reminded me that Don Bailey would be arriving shortly. T.W. had just picked him up from the Ashville airport, which was a twenty-minute drive from Montreat. During their ride, T.W. would brief Bailey on the necessary preparations for Billy's press conference prior to the start of the Jackson Crusade.

As we awaited Don's arrival, I asked Billy how he had assembled his original team. I had known of his early evangelistic work with Cliff Barrows and George Beverly Shea, but knew little of why he had chosen some of his other key people, like his boyhood friends, the Wilson brothers. Billy told me that when he first began to travel extensively, he asked Grady Wilson to accompany him. Grady was a born storyteller and had a relaxing influence on Billy at the end of a strenuous day. He was also a counselor of great common sense and intuitive wisdom. Later, when Grady became busy with his own burgeoning evangelistic schedule within the organization, Billy called upon T.W. to be at his side during his travels.

A number of other major staff members came from the Youth for Christ movement. As a leader of this organization, Graham came into contact with many of its local directors. One of them, the brilliant and energetic George Wilson, went from being director of Minneapolis Youth for Christ to the business manager of the nascent Billy Graham Evangelistic Association. Sterling Huston, who served as Graham's team director for North America, once headed the Youth for Christ movement in Rochester, New York.

What was especially impressive about the members of Graham's staff—beyond their competence, capabilities, and positive and endearing personalities—was their loyalty to the evangelist. Most if not all members of the original team could have formed their own groups long ago, but chose instead to remain with Graham. Cliff Barrows claimed that one of the main reasons he stayed with Billy all of these years was that they were very compatible—in all of their years together, they never had one serious disagreement. Cliff, like most of Graham's staff, also believed that Billy had a special calling, one in which he delighted in sharing.

And Graham has always been a staff-friendly leader. When interacting with his team, he is neither interested in flattery nor in staff members who passively agree with him. He welcomes honest and frank discussions with people who are not afraid to express their opinions.

The BGEA has grown into a tremendous entity, a far cry from the early days when Billy, Bev Shea, Grady Wilson, and Cliff and Billie Barrows would hop across the country to hold meetings in places like Pontiac, Michigan, and Kearny, Nebraska. Billy confessed that, unfortunately, this growth made it impossible to stay in close touch with all of the members of his organization, but he was genuinely interested in their welfare and morale. Whenever he learned that someone had a special need or was having a specific problem, he took a keen and personal interest.

Billy also kept in touch with families of team members, and extended himself whenever he could. For instance, I learned some stories about the family of Howard Jones, the first black evangelist to be appointed by Graham. Jones's son David invited Graham to speak at his college commencement. Although Graham had to decline the invitation, he wrote David a long letter, advising him about the ministry in the same fashion that Paul had written to Timothy.

On another occasion, Graham had the opportunity to speak with Mrs. Jones. During their conversation, she told him of her involvement in a teaching program for mentally retarded children. Graham, who had tremendous curiosity on almost every subject, was very interested in the program, which he discussed with her at length. Some months later, Billy spoke at the dedication of a new center in Ohio for the mentally retarded at Mrs. Jones's request.

BILLY AND THE PRESS

Our conversation was suddenly interrupted when Don Bailey and T.W. entered the room. Before joining the BGEA, Bailey was a journalist. He was a friendly man who exuded an air of competence. In Jackson, I would be impressed by both his coolness under pressure and unfailing courtesy toward the press.

Billy motioned for Don and T.W. to sit, but T.W. excused himself, explaining that he had a deskload of correspondence to answer and about twenty telephone calls to make. As soon as Don settled into a chair, Billy asked how the plans for the crusade's press coverage were coming along, to which Bailey replied that everything was going smoothly. Don told Billy that the wire services would, of course, pick up anything of national interest, but that he expected only a handful of out-of-state reporters. On the other hand, due to significant advance interest in the crusade, he anticipated excellent local and statewide coverage.

Jackson, Mississippi, which is rife with evangelical Christians, is not one of the most difficult places in the world for Billy to be understood and appreciated. And as the geographic outreach of the crusade extended into Alabama, Tennessee, and Louisiana, the meetings in Jackson would attract many of the already interested, if not the converted. It was the genuine Bible Belt, and Don Bailey wouldn't have to worry too much about suspicious reporters in search of a juicy Graham story. In spite of this, he still took his work at the Jackson sessions as seriously as he would for a crusade in hostile territory.

Bailey's attitude was typical of Graham's people; he did not compromise his standards. A seasoned professional who had been at this for years, Don knew which problems to anticipate and was prepared for all contingencies. He also knew that when dealing with the media, his boss was one of the best in the business. Unlike many other public relations specialists, who had to create and then sustain a public figure's image, Don's chief responsibility was to execute sound public relations. Graham himself was one of the world's most adept and experienced public relations men. *He* set the tone; *he* made the news. It was then Don's responsibility to ensure that Billy's words were accurately and efficiently communicated.

That afternoon, Don brought along some interview requests from local Jackson television, radio, and print outlets. In addition, he asked Billy if a Swedish television crew could tape an interview with him for a special it was preparing. Billy agreed to do as many interviews as could fit into his ever-tightening schedule.

Don and his associate Arthur Matthews had already spent two days in Jackson, meeting with reporters and media executives. Don briefed Billy on the local scene, informing him where in the stadium the media would be seated, as well as the location of the team's media headquarters in their hotel. He had already scheduled a number of radio and television appearances for Billy and the members of his team, and Jackson's morning and evening newspapers were expected to carry front-page stories on each day of the crusade.

When Don and Billy concluded their business, Don gathered his paperwork together, shook hands with the evangelist, and left.

HOUR OF DECISION

A few minutes later, T.W. appeared in the doorway to ask Billy when he would be able to get to radio station WFGM in Black Mountain for a taping of the *Hour of Decision*. WFGM and WMIT-FM comprised the Blue Ridge Broadcasting Corporation, an adjunct of the Graham ministry. Both stations featured religious programs and inspirational music. Billy told T.W. that he would be there the next morning, and the staff should be prepared to tape two programs. He wanted to get ahead of his taping schedule to free up some time to work on a magazine article.

Graham took the *Hour of Decision* radio program very, very seriously. In a real sense, this program, which was named by Ruth and first aired in 1950, was the foundation of Graham's national ministry, spurring the formation of the Billy Graham Evangelistic Association. The idea for the program originated with two advertising executives, Walter Bennett and Fred Dienert. Both recognized the need for Billy to preach his message to a national radio audience. Although the *Hour of Decision* would soon become the most listened to religious broadcast in America—eliciting more mail response than any other single aspect of the Graham ministry—its success was hardly predictable as Billy struggled to find the money with which to fund the initial thirteen-week commitment.

In the early days, Graham's radio messages reflected the nation's preoccupation with the threat of communism—real or imagined. Graham often attacked that political system, warning that the Soviets were preparing to take over America's vital institutions. As the years passed and the political and social climate changed, Graham turned away from the communist menace, directing his attention instead to the effects of living in a complex and ever-changing society.

Salvation through Christ, always at the heart of his message, was becoming a clarion call to America. At the same time, Graham analyzed other issues that were capturing the public's attention—racial tension, student unrest, liberation movements, national lifestyle, and the breakdown of the family. These issues were discussed on the *Hour of Decision* as symptomatic of a deeper malaise that affected society, bringing greater clarity to Graham's radio preaching.

I have long been impressed with the clarity, consistency, and professionalism of the *Hour of Decision*. And there was no doubt that Billy regarded it as a vital part of his ministry.

CORRESPONDENCE

Stephanie Wills came into the living room, reminding Graham that he had to dictate several important letters that needed to go out in the evening mail. Billy usually wrote twenty or so letters a day—only the tip of the iceberg of his ministry-related correspondence.

The BGEA headquarters received thousands of letters each week, the bulk of which included contributions. Following a national telecast, the volume was significantly higher. These letters were answered through an automated process. Billy also received a lot of personal mail, which ranged from speaking invitations to letters seeking his advice on personal matters. His personally written correspondence covered a wide range of subjects and was often addressed to dignitaries, well-known personalities, and people who were involved with an activity in which he had a special interest. On occasion, he also wrote to everyday people with specific issues or problems.

As it was impossible for Graham to respond to the majority of letters seeking his advice on personal matters, his staff answered this mail. Each response included general guidance and information that Billy had provided for the type of advice being sought. No letter was ever sent out under Billy's signature unless he had personally dictated it. Billy told me that when telegrams were still a common means of communication, he received thousands of them annually. He recalled one incredible incident that took place on November 2, 1964. On that day, an avalanche of 60,000 telegrams arrived urging Billy to endorse Barry Goldwater, the Republican presidential candidate!

Billy also spent a good part of most days on the telephone. He kept in touch with the various offices of his worldwide organization, located in places like Buenos Aires, Argentina, and Sydney, Australia. He also spoke at least once with his headquarters in Minneapolis. Billy initiated most of the calls. Staff members, realizing the complexity of his schedule, called him with only the most urgent matters. Billy received hundreds of local and long-distance calls every day at the various offices—many from distraught people who simply wanted to talk to him. All of the calls were screened. In Billy's Montreat office, calls were also screened twenty-four hours a day.

PREPARING SERMONS

As mid-afternoon drew near, Billy needed some quiet time to work on his correspondence, so I stepped outside and took in the lovely view from the mountaintop. Montreat, where his nearby neighbors were also close friends and associates, was Billy's refuge from the press of outside forces and events—a place where he could truly relax. He read on the screened-in porch of his mountain home, jogged through his rustic surroundings, and relaxed in his small thermal bath. I envied Graham this retreat, far from the noise of the city and concerns of the everyday world.

In addition to preparing his radio sermons and working on his correspondence, Billy also outlined the messages he would be delivering during the upcoming Jackson Crusade. He wasn't exactly starting from scratch—after all, he had spent decades preaching. There were very few themes or subjects he had not already treated or at least touched on. Each sermon in Jackson was to take about thirty-five minutes to deliver—a far cry from the sermons of his early crusades, which often ran over an hour. The strength of Billy's sermons has always been in their messages, which have an incredible effect on diverse audiences. If the Jackson Crusade proved typical, Billy was likely to devote his individual sermons to the problems of youth, family life, the Second Coming of Christ, and critical world issues.

A keen student of history, Billy quoted from news magazines, best-selling books, and recognized authorities in various fields when preaching. His words generally reflected an informed perception of reality, and were neither political nor socially provocative. In fact, some of Billy's critics have accused him of being "simplistic" in his approach to human problems. I asked Billy if he was bothered by this suggestion that his preaching lacked depth. He responded:

> No. My preaching is based on the proposition that the evangelist must articulate a message capable of reaching as broad a base of people as possible. This message must have a sense of urgency and it must articulate in the clearest terms the basic Gospel message of salvation through Christ.

From Billy's perspective, there was little purpose in giving a talk in which the Gospel was not the major thread. Even on those rare occasions when he addressed a group that did not expect or welcome a crusade-type message, he quoted the Scriptures and articulated his personal testimony of the meaning of faith in Christ. By doing this, in *New Testament* terminology, he has "sown the seed," fulfilling his calling as an evangelist to proclaim the Good News of salvation.

Billy was troubled that only a few outstanding preachers were active in this day and age. He told me that the same five or six clergymen were called upon to speak at the major church conferences, adding that "When Bishop Arthur Moore [a leading Methodist] was alive, he was in great demand, but today there were few men who could preach the way he did."

A CAREFUL STUDENT

Billy, who served on the board of nearby Montreat-Anderson College and addressed the entire student body on several occasions, liked to invite a dozen or so students to come up to the house for an evening of intense and lively discussion. Long interested in education and student life, Billy sensed his own lack of formal training as he never went beyond obtaining his bachelor's degree.

Interestingly, although he has preached to more people than any other human being, Billy does not have a graduate degree in theology—regarded as one of his virtues by writer and seminary professor Harold Lindsell. Lindsell believed the seminary experience could dull a person's evangelistic zeal and lessen the priority of spreading the Gospel message. He argued that the great nineteenth- and twentieth-century American evangelists did not have conventional theological backgrounds. He did add that although Graham was without this degree, he has always been a keen and careful student, who supplemented his Bible education over the years with a wide range of critical readings. Billy also had the gift of being able to extract information from informed people; he was a great questioner and could get to the core of an issue, seldom forgetting what he learned.

Because of his high regard for the value of higher education, Billy gave a significant portion of his annual tithe to Christian colleges and seminaries. He told me that although his early educational experiences had occurred within the narrow settings of Bob Jones College and the Florida Bible Institute, the time he spent at these schools had not been without some value.

At Bob Jones College, for instance, he said he learned the dangers inherent in an ultra-fundamentalist worldview—one in which the possibility of Christian charity would be shut off and the horizons of one's ministry limited. While at the Florida Bible Institute, he gained a deeper spiritual life; it was there that he began the systematic study of Scriptures that would become an unchanging part of his daily routine. It was also at the Institute that the inherent power of his preaching became evident and would take him from the swamps of Florida and backwoods churches to major cities throughout the world.

It was while studying at Wheaton College, however, that Billy would come into contact with believers who pursued a wide range of secular subjects without fear of compromising, or losing, their faith. At Wheaton, Billy would be known as a man with a tremendous interest in soul winning. One friend recalled how most mornings his eyes were red from lack of sleep, his expression bearing evidence to the hours spent reading the Bible and in praying. And Billy also preached publicly in the Wheaton area, first at the Tabernacle Church and then at the Baptist church in Western Springs, Illinois.

CONTRIBUTIONS OF GEORGE WILSON

As I sat in the living room, jotting down notes, George Wilson, the executive vice president of the BGEA, stopped by. A native of North Dakota, Wilson became acquainted with Graham when both men were affiliated with Youth for Christ. From 1947 to 1950, Wilson served as business manager of Northwestern Schools. Then in 1950, when the *Hour of Decision* went on the air, Billy asked George to set up an entity to handle the funds needed to sustain the radio program. Billy had him rent a small office and borrow, rather than purchase, furniture and office machines, as "We might not be on the air more than thirteen weeks."

Operating from a cramped, 600-square-foot space in Minneapolis, Wilson set about organizing what became one of the most efficiently run religious operations in the world. Looking back at those early years, Wilson told me, "I think I would have been scared to death if I'd have known it was going to develop to the extent it has."

George Wilson described the BGEA as "business-like, but not operating like a business." Several years earlier, a group of management experts touring the Minneapolis headquarters were surprised at the constant flurry of activity. One of them remarked to Wilson, "My, all of these people are actually *working*." Replying, Wilson said that all of those workers, realizing that they were partners with Billy Graham in his ministry, had a special motivation for putting in a sixty-minute hour.

During his tenure as chief of the Graham organization's business operations, Wilson was both innovative and highly successful. The BGEA was considered the most cost-effective nonprofit organization in the United States. Despite its low overhead, the BGEA has always been a first-class operation. Its offices are modern and contain the most up-to-date equipment.

World Wide Pictures had distributed its films for years through traveling representatives. A rep would bring a film to a local church, show it, and then receive a goodwill offering from the congregation. Then Wilson determined that there would be considerable savings in salary, travel, and living costs if the films were distributed on a rental basis. Furthermore, World Wide Pictures would have better control over its prints, and eliminate the need to purchase costly projectors.

The Graham organization works on a very strict budget. Billy, who is involved in every major policy decision, does not believe in deficit financing. As one of his close associates told me, "Billy is an evangelist first, but he is also one of the best businessmen I know." Graham has a tremendous sense of responsibility to the multitudes of people who contribute money to his organization, and will not allow any funds to be wasted on frivolous or unproductive projects. The BGEA has a strong board of directors, which meets two times a year. In between these meetings, an executive committee, which convenes every six weeks, directs the organization.

BREAKDOWN OF THE FAMILY

When Stephanie Wills returned, she handed Billy several drafts of his syndicated newspaper column, *My Answer*, which appeared in more than 300 newspapers. In it, Billy answered questions that had been sent in by readers. In the column he worked on that afternoon, the questions dealt with alcoholism, disobedient children, and the problems of aging.

Billy told me that although he was concerned about a great number of issues, he was particularly troubled by the apparent disintegration of the American family. It was the theme of many of his sermons and messages in his newspaper column. Having been brought up in a warm but strict atmosphere in which his parents provided a secure setting, Billy always described his mother and father in proud and loving terms.

Billy was also aware that due to his many obligations, his own children did not have the benefit of his constant presence as they came of age. Ruth had to fulfill two parental roles for long periods of time. When the Grahams' daughter Bunny spoke to *Good Housekeeping* about Ruth's contributions to her father's work, she stated that she had "never heard a cross word" uttered between her parents. She also said that "without her, Daddy could never have done what he's done. Just imagine if he had a wife nagging him on the phone every night, saying, 'Why aren't you home?' or 'The water pipes just burst.'"

THE NEED TO PREACH SIMPLY

Billy, a great student of the Bible, knows all of its themes and currents. He cannot, however, preach on many aspects of the Scriptures; as an evangelist, his ministry is principally one of reductionism. This does not mean that his preaching and ministry are simplistic. Rather, he has to make the *New Testament* account of Jesus's life and death the core of his message. Billy's sermons are not meant for the seminary lecture hall or for gatherings of long-time believers; his mission is to proclaim the Gospel in as simple, relevant, and forceful a manner as possible. He has to be able to reach the average man clearly and succinctly, but with intense feeling and verve.

Billy has always felt a sense of frustration over this because, as he told me, he would love to preach on many Biblical subjects; but that is not the way of the evangelist. From my point of view though, the great virtue in Billy's continuous, systematic study of the Bible was the assurance and authority it brought to his preaching. The Bible was the foundation of Billy's ministry; it was his compass, his focal point. Yet, Billy did not fall into the trap that ensnared so many other well-meaning evangelists—he was not a Biblicist; he did not limit the experiential world to the Bible, nor did he use the Scriptures as something magical. And while he truly believed the Bible was the inspired word of God, he knew that, unless activated by a man's life, the teachings of the Scriptures were meaningless in a world that looks to a person's deeds for proof of one's words.

BILLY AND BOOKS

At one point in our conversation, Billy asked me about our

mutual interest—writing. Before long he had me talking at great length and in considerable detail about my work habits, as well as the pros and cons of being represented by a literary agent. Billy didn't have an agent; an attorney in New York represented him in dealings with his publisher.

As we talked, I noticed a copy of *Eleanor: The Years Alone* on the coffee table, and I ask about his reading habits. I learned that he read *The New York Times* and *The Washington Post* daily. He had just finished reading *Jaws* and the *Gulag Archipelago*. He also confessed that often, because of time constraints, he didn't read a book all the way through. So whenever Ruth or one of his friends suggested a book, they often marked the portions they believed would be of particular interest to him.

Billy told me of his meeting with Alexander Solzhenitsyn, the exiled Russian author of *Gulag Archipelago*. Billy learned that the Nobel Prize winner wanted to see him. A week later, when he was in Europe on business, Billy flew to Stockholm and spent two hours with Solzhenitsyn, who wanted to know about religious conditions in the United States and other areas of the world. Billy learned the status of religion in the Soviet Union.

Such meetings were not unusual for Billy; very often he was approached by major personalities and celebrities who wanted to speak with him or share a particular problem or concern. Throughout his career, he had been received by leading political figures, many of whom viewed Billy as having a prophetic voice, even when they disagreed with his Christian outlook.

American politicians were especially interested in cultivating relationships and being seen with Billy. In 1972, a presidential election year, Billy attended the groundbreaking for the Lyndon Johnson Library in Texas, and several would-be Democratic Party candidates—including Hubert Humphrey, Henry Jackson, and George McGovern—sought him out and managed to be photographed with him.

Soon, our discussion led me to ask Billy how he worked on his books, several of which have been major bestsellers. He said that normally, he wrote at home in the comfort of his small study. But there were also times when he found himself working on his projects on airplanes and in hotel rooms. At the time of our meeting, he was working on *Angels*, some of which he had written at a friend's vacation home in Mexico. But even while he was there, his writing was interrupted by phone calls and other correspondence. He told me how much he enjoyed working on that particular project; that he loved digging into a subject and researching it thoroughly. *Angels* was first published in 1975, and sold over 1 million copies in the first three months it was available.

RELATIONSHIPS WITH PRESIDENTS

While Billy's ministry has been directed at bringing souls to Christ, his status as one of the world's most admired and influential people has brought him into contact with U.S. presidents and scores of world leaders.

In his relationships with political figures, particularly American presidents, from Harry Truman to George W. Bush, Billy has acted more as a spiritual adviser and friend than as a spokesman for a specific political agenda. The presidents understood that Graham had positions on major issues, which would come up in private conversation. They also knew that Billy would not betray their confidences. This was a lesson the evangelist learned following his first meeting with a chief executive; he provoked President Truman's ire by giving reporters a detailed account of their meeting in the Oval Office.

Graham enjoyed a warm friendship—almost of a father-son nature—with Truman's successor, Dwight D. Eisenhower. The evangelist was not particularly close to John F. Kennedy, with whom he occasionally golfed. He was, however, quite friendly with Lyndon Johnson, and spent many hours with the president and his family in both Washington and Texas.

Billy and Johnson's successor, Richard Nixon, had a warm, if complex, relationship. The two men, who enjoyed each other's company, first met in 1950. The evangelist expressed strong support for Nixon in 1968 and 1972, but reacted strongly to the Watergate affair, even writing an article that appeared on the Op Ed page in *The New York Times*. The article criticized Nixon's approach to the unfolding scandal. Yet, Graham supported Gerald Ford's decision to pardon Nixon, and he remained close to his old friend during the ex-president's years in California and New Jersey.

Graham was friendly with all of Nixon's successors, spending time with them in prayer, counseling, and fellowship. As Billy's stature grew as a beloved national icon, presidents often called on him to speak at public events. Most noteworthy in this regard were the messages of consolation and hope he delivered at the memorial services following the Oklahoma City bombing in 1995, and the September 11, 2001, attacks on the Pentagon and World Trade Center.

A MASTER OF DETERMINATION

As I read over my notes, Billy and George Wilson talked about the mail response to a completed series of telecasts. At that time, the cost of one nationwide telecast was around $250,000. The men discussed how it was becoming increasingly difficult to raise that kind of money, despite the fact that the average gift to the BGEA had risen from $5 in 1973 to $8 in 1974.

During the mid-1970s, due to the long-term inflationary spiral, the fundraising dollar was becoming harder to come by and less useful when it was finally brought in. This prompted Billy to send out a special letter, asking long-time contributors to give more. In spite of the reality of this financial strain, Billy did not appear uneasy. When I met George Wilson a few months later at the 1975 Jackson Crusade, we talked about Billy's characteristically calm demeanor in spite of these possible troubles. Wilson attributed this lack of anxiety to his strong faith. He told me, "Every so often, Billy comes up with programs that just don't seem feasible, but you see the hand of the Lord in it—you know that whatever program he is going to project, the Lord has led him to it in the hours of the night."

Indeed, one of the most arresting aspects of Billy's personality is his capacity to think big, to attempt programs that others would not deem possible. The launching of the *Hour of Decision* radio broadcast; the introduction of televised crusades; the initiation of *Decision* magazine, currently published in four English-language editions, six foreign languages, and Braille; and the development of a major film subsidiary were all actions that men of less vision, drive, and, perhaps, faith, would not have attempted. The best-known and most successful evangelist of his time, Billy has always been very conscious of his role as head of the BGEA. He has never shied away from his responsibilities and, in a sense, has always relished the daily challenges.

Afterward, Billy told me of his great affection and respect for George Wilson, saying, "It is so helpful to have someone like George in charge of the business side of my activities. He is reliable, has great integrity, and he walks with God." On a lighter note, Billy also told me of the time he called Wilson at home from Frankfurt, Germany. "When George answered, he sounded sleepy," Billy recalled. "I asked him why he was so groggy, and he replied, 'You would be tired too if someone called you at four o'clock in the morning!' It seemed I did not take into account the six-hour time difference between Frankfurt and Minneapolis when I made the call."

THE HIDING PLACE

The ringing of the telephone interrupted Billy's reminiscences of Wilson. It was T.W., reporting that the latest rushes of the World Wide Pictures film *The Hiding Place* were ready for viewing.

During our drive back to the office, Billy told me a little about the movie, which was based on a best-selling book of the same name. It related the dramatic experiences of Corrie ten Boom and her family during World War II, when Corrie's home in Haarlem, the Netherlands, became a refuge for hundreds of Jews seeking to escape Hitler's extermination campaign.

The ten Boom family's rescue efforts were eventually discovered, and Corrie and her sister, Betsie, were sent to the infamous Ravensbrück concentration camp, where Betsie died. One week before the women in her barracks were scheduled to be put to death, Corrie was released due to a clerical error by her Nazi captors. Emerging from Ravensbrück with deep faith—one that sustained her during her time of captivity—Corrie recalled a dream Betsie had had shortly before her death. In it, the two sisters went into the world to tell of their faith, which brought victory over hate, fear, and discouragement. At the heart of their desire to spread their beliefs was Betsie's conviction that "There is no pit so deep, and no darkness so black, that the love of God cannot triumph over it." Billy and Corrie ten Boom had been friends for many years. She often appeared at crusade meetings and was a frequent guest in the Graham home.

As we drove down the mountain, Billy told me that Corrie, who was eighty-four years old, had a worldwide speaking ministry. She also headed a foundation, published a monthly magazine, and was in great demand by young people as a counselor. Her activities were nothing short of amazing, considering her age.

The movie, which featured major Hollywood actors, cost close to $2 million to produce. At the time, it was the most ambitious film project undertaken by the Graham organization. It was also very close to Billy's heart. When I asked why he had put so much effort into *The Hiding Place*, he replied that the theme of Christians helping Jews in a period of crisis was very timely, given the current situation in the world. Elaborating, he said:

> I am worried about the status of the Jews. The oil situation and attacks on the Judeo-Christian tradition are signs that things could go badly for the Jewish people. I hope this film will remind Christians of their responsibility toward the Jews.

These words seemed to echo those of Corrie's father. When his pastor asked why he was risking his family's safety and security for the Jews. Mr. ten Boom replied, "It will be an honor for me to give my life for God's ancient people."

When we reached the office and made our way to the screening room, we were met by T.W., who briefed Billy on the status of the production. The film was almost finished and a rough cut would be ready in about three weeks. After viewing the movie that afternoon, some important decisions had to be made concerning the film's length and final scenes. We would be watching footage of two possible endings. In one, the real Corrie was seen seated in her old house in Haarlem. The other ending had a freeze frame of actress Jeannette Clift, who portrayed Corrie, leaving Ravensbrück.

Unlike most of the staff members of World Wide Pictures, Billy had always leaned toward the real Corrie ending, and his opinion was confirmed after viewing the rushes. As soon as the film ended and the lights came up, he picked up the telephone and placed a call to Bill Brown, a long-time team member and then-president of World Wide Pictures. Billy told him how much he enjoyed the scenes he had just watched, and would like to go with the real-life ending.

Brown then asked Billy if he was satisfied with the length of the film, which was over two-and-a-half hours. Most commercially distributed features ran about two hours, which theater owners preferred because it meant they could get in an extra showing during the course of a normal day. Billy, however, was reluctant to make any cuts, which he strongly believed would dilute the film's message. And while there may have been several potential solutions to remedy the length problem, once Billy made his decision, the matter was settled.

I was struck both by Billy's familiarity with film-industry terms and his grasp of the technical and artistic aspects of film-making. Furthermore, as an astute businessman, he was also aware of the financial realities of distribution, theater rentals, ticket pricing, and promotion. There was no doubt that the Graham organization would be going all out to make *The Hiding Place* a success. Everybody I spoke with that day believed in the film and was carried along by Billy's enthusiasm and guidance.

A LIFETIME OF HARD WORK

As I continued to observe Billy that day, I became increasingly impressed by his capacity for hard work—a quality he showed from the time he was a young boy. Growing up on a dairy farm, he was responsible for a daily routine of dull and difficult chores. During high school, he worked summers as a Fuller Brush salesman, and came to be regarded as one of the best in the North Carolina region. While attending the Florida Bible Institute, he earned money by washing dishes in the school cafeteria. At Wheaton, he supplemented his income by moving furniture. In addition, Billy devoted many hours to Bible study, meditation, and prayer, so much so that his friends wondered how he found the time to preach and to court Ruth Bell.

During the growth of his ministry, Billy pursued a schedule that would tax the energies of most men, yet he never entertained the idea of stopping—of resting on his considerable accomplishments. Billy's good friend and confidante Harold Lindsell has said, "Billy would go crazy if he had to sit still for two weeks. If he went to a cloister, it would cease to be a cloister; it would become a beehive." It's simply that Billy's mind is always in high gear, and he is eager to absorb and catalogue any information concerning both his organization and the outside world. He is also a notoriously poor sleeper.

Perhaps the only limitation of his relentless drive toward work was his struggle with high blood pressure. Everyone around Billy urged him to slow down, to cut his schedule. They encouraged him to make more time for golf and other forms of recreation. But Billy was driven by his sense of responsibility, first to the countless people who did not share his spiritual worldview, and then to the organization he built and to those who worked for him.

When I asked Billy if he had given any thought to the possibility of retiring in the near future, as do many people in their late fifties, he said that he had no such plans. He said, "The needs of the world are so great, the workers so few and fragmented." He continued, "Yet, I also believe we are on the verge of a major spir-itual breakthrough, and I want to share in this movement of God in history."

It was obvious that work was a tonic for Billy, a great satis-faction. Throughout the day, as I observed him speaking on the telephone, chatting with Stephanie and T.W., or looking through a batch of mail, there was a zestfulness about him. I got the impression that to him nothing was routine; everything was of genuine interest. When I mentioned my impression to Billy, he responded by saying that he regarded each new day as a chal-lenge, an opportunity to serve God and add to the building of His kingdom. He exuded an air of optimism, and was blessed with a faith that enabled him to perceive the ugly side of human exis-tence while believing in the ultimate wisdom of God's plan for mankind.

BACK AT HOME

The afternoon light was fading when we left the office. T.W. walked us out. He then shook my hand and told me he'd come back to the house later that evening to drive me back to the office to pick up my car.

The ride up the mountain was fairly quiet. Billy may have been thinking about the rushes he had just viewed. Or, perhaps, he was simply enjoying the gorgeous scenery of the mountain-side. I broke into his thoughts, asking about the day's remaining agenda. The schedule was flexible from that point on.

When we reached the house, the fireplace was lit and Ruth was busy in the kitchen preparing Billy's favorite meal—potatoes baked in a wood-burning stove, grilled steak, tossed salad, and coffee. Ruth enjoyed working in the kitchen. Beatrice Long, the Graham's maid of twenty-five years, was semi-retired and came in only a few days a week. The Grahams also employed George and Corrine Burgin, who managed the household when Ruth or Billy were away.

When she heard us come into the house, Ruth emerged from

the kitchen and greeted us with a warm smile and bright hello. Billy introduced us, and she graciously shook my hand and told me how pleased she was that I would be staying for dinner. She was, as her housemother at Wheaton College described her in 1943, "Very attractive, beautiful to look at and [has] excellent taste in dress. . . . And she has the intellectual qualities to make a success in any work she would choose to undertake." As an adult, Ruth developed into a well-rounded and mature person. Not only was she instrumental in maintaining their household and raising their children, she was a great help to her husband. Furthermore, she emerged as a Christian leader in her own right—respected throughout the world and a favored speaker at many women's gatherings. In the years since their children were married and established in their own homes, Ruth was free to travel with Billy. I learned that she would be joining her husband on his swing through Asia later that year.

As Ruth finished preparing dinner, Billy and I moved into the den, where he placed some logs on the already roaring fire. He then relaxed in a comfortable-looking easy chair, and immediately began speaking about his wife. It was obvious that he was proud of her as he spoke of one of her latest involvements. Ruth served as one of the organizers of a task force aimed at mobilizing Protestant women "in defense of life." Its goal was to bring increased awareness to right-to-life issues. The group would be hosting a conference at the Montreat Conference Center in a few months.

Since he had just broached the subject of women and women's rights, I ask his views on women's liberation. It was the 1970s, and this was a hotly debated issue. He was very emphatic in stating that there should be equal opportunity for women, but questioned whether the women's movement might be fostering confusion regarding male and female roles. He said, "I think a woman ought to be proud to be a woman and a man ought to be proud to be a man; the man must always remember that his wife is not an object but a person."

I then suggested that some feminists believed that organized religion was oppressive to women in terms of its teaching and practices. Taking issue with that premise, Billy said:

> If you go into areas of the world where Christianity is not important, or Judaism has never gone, you'll find the woman in a very inferior position. What is more, the Judeo-Christian tradition has formulated the best basis I know for relationships between the sexes. The Bible teaches each mate respect for the other and establishes principles which lead to happy and productive family living.

A RELAXING EVENING

Ruth called us to dinner. Billy and Ruth were very much at ease with having me at their dinner table. There wasn't the slightest hint of pretension or self-importance as they spoke of their children, an upcoming trip, the need for Billy to replace a worn-out jacket, and the possibility of riding over to Charlotte the next day to have lunch with the Grady Wilsons. Our relaxed conversation was not unlike those being conducted at dinner tables all over the United States.

When dinner was just about over, the phone rang. It was the White House, calling to confirm Billy's appointment with President Ford. I later learned that during their meeting, the two men would spend five hours together, praying, reading the Scriptures, and discussing a wide range of current issues.

Billy asked if I would like to join him for a walk along the hillside. As we stepped outside, I breathed in the clean evening air; the first stars of evening were visible and appeared close enough to touch. As I walked alongside this world-famous religious leader and took in the magnificent mountain view under the darkening star-studded sky, I felt especially inconsequential— and my thoughts leaned toward the spiritual. I thought about the world and Billy's belief that its end was at hand. It was a theme he had spoken of numerous times. I asked if he really believed that events were coming to a head. He replied:

Well, it's, of course, foolish to fix dates. Jesus warned against it. Medieval literature is filled with doomsday prophecies—Luther said he might live to see the end of his age, John Wesley expected the final overthrow of the beast in 1836. But I do believe we are living in the last days, and that we've been living in the last days for a long time. I'm convinced that we're moving toward that final day, the climactic moment when Christ will come and set up a new world and the Kingdom of God will prevail.

Billy's position on the Second Coming of Christ has not led him into exaggerated pietism or a total sense of hopelessness regarding what can be accomplished on the spiritual, moral, and social levels. Armed with the conviction that at the proper moment, God's eternal plan will be realized, he will continue to preach and to direct his organization. He is, however, very emphatic about the kind of victory God will ultimately achieve:

And all the evil systems of this world, all the lying, cheating, hating, injustice, and corruption are going to come to an end. But they cannot come to an end through any form of government the world has ever known. Every type of government has been permeated with corruption, evil, and greed, but there's one type we have not tried. That is theocracy, with Christ on the throne and the nations of the world confessing Him. Then, and only then, can the world be free of the bondage of sin and be set free, to have peace, because He is the Prince of Peace. And I feel this about America. I love America, but I am not an ambassador for America. I represent a higher power. I am an ambassador for Christ, and someday His flag will wave over every nation of the world.

We walked in silence for a while, and I thought about Billy's words. He broke the silence, telling me how happy he was to be at home and how much he looked forward to the day when he would be able to spend months, rather than days or weeks, in Montreat. I asked him what activities he would pursue if he had a more relaxed lifestyle. He answered that he would like to devote more time to study and writing, and perhaps teach at a seminary or university. But this was wishful thinking, as we both knew that Billy's schedule for the next eighteen months was totally filled. I thought back to Cliff Barrows' words: "I don't imagine the time will ever come when Billy will say, 'Well, the hay is in the barn and I can sit back and relax.'"

At around 9:00, the evening air began to turn chilly, so we returned to the house, where the conversation turned to Billy's *Angels* manuscript. He had begun working on the project the previous Christmas and had just finished the final chapter a week before my visit. I asked why he became interested in writing an entire book on such an esoteric subject. He responded by saying:

> When I started to research the subject, I found that very little had been written on angels. There are a lot of books on demons and devils and the occult, and you'd almost think the devil is going to win the whole thing, But God has principalities and powers at his command, and they are at the disposal of Christians, and they are going to come with drawn swords and flaming chariots and are going to win the battle against the devil and his forces.

Billy mentioned that he still had to go over the second draft of the manuscript and finalize some of the information before submitting it to his editor. Knowing that T.W. wouldn't be picking me up for another two hours, I told him that if he wanted to work on it that night while I was there, it would be fine. It would also give me some quiet time and an opportunity to organize my own notes. He gratefully accepted my offer and excused himself to his study. About an hour later, he emerged and came into the kitchen, where I had been working at the table. He asked if I would like to watch a detective thriller on television with him and Ruth. Although he liked to watch the news and documentaries, Billy was not really a television fan—more often than not he relaxed by reading or listening to records. But occasionally, television was a mild and welcome distraction, a pastime he and Ruth enjoyed together.

As Billy and Ruth, holding hands, sat together on a small couch facing their television set, their deep love for one another was evident. They had journeyed a long way since their first date, a recital of Handel's *Messiah,* which they attended one snowy Sunday during their days at Wheaton College. And in all the days they have been together and in all the months they have been apart, they have, by act and example, contributed immeasurably to the well-being of multitudes of people. And they have many miles to go before they sleep.

Just as the detective thriller reached its denouement, T.W. arrived at the house. I gathered up my notes and said my good-byes. As Billy and Ruth walked me to the door, I thanked them for their hospitality and reminded Billy that I would soon be seeing him in Jackson.

4

Early Morning in Jackson

IT WAS JUST AFTER 7:00 ON A WARM and sunny spring morning in 1975, and Jackson, Mississippi, the capital of the Deep South, was coming alive. At the Municipal Airport, the day's first Eastern Airlines jet rolled down the runway on its way to Atlanta. A few miles further south, Bill C. Franklin delivered mail on his suburban route. At his modern ranch on Roebuck Drive, Tom Bailey just finished his first cup of coffee of the day, before driving to the Mississippi State Bank, where he was vice president. In a nearby shopping center, Sarah Herndon rang up some items at a supermarket checkout counter. The cooks at Morrison's Cafeteria hustled to accommodate the normal breakfast traffic, and at police headquarters, a number of officers headed toward their patrol cars and motorcycles as they began their day shift. Jimmy and Carol Wheatly ran, as they usually did, to catch the bus that took them to Parkside Junior High School. And in the intensive care unit of the University Medical Center, Linda May Rogers carefully monitored the vital signs of an Ellis Avenue insurance salesman who had suffered a heart attack during the night.

At the Holiday Inn on North Frontage Road, Billy Graham, on his first visit to Jackson in twenty-three years, munched on a piece of toast and watched the *Today Show* news report from his top-floor suite. There were many things this visitor could have been doing on this lovely morning—drive the seven miles to the downtown area and tour the state capitol, head to the museum that housed precious artifacts from the prebellum South, or stop along the Ross Barnett Reservoir with some fishing gear to see if the catfish and walleyes were in a biting mood. But he didn't have time for any of these pleasant diversions.

Billy walked over to the desk in the corner of his suite, sat down, and read from a well-thumbed copy of the *Living Bible*. Then, with the day's portion of the Scriptures perused and absorbed, he bowed his head and meditated. Billy contemplated many concerns that were in his heart, as well as the multitude of questions that had been asked of him by people seeking his advice. He also thought about the reason he left his beautiful mountain country home in western North Carolina to hold a crusade in Jackson. As he considered the tasks and responsibilities that awaited him that day, he was humbled. And then, as he did each day of his life, he asked God for strength, wisdom, and blessing upon his ministry.

As Billy studied and prayed in Jackson that morning, the switchboard in his Minneapolis headquarters had already begun to light up with the first of many hundreds of calls that would come in during the day; a secretary in his Paris office typed a letter to an Antwerp clergyman who had requested a meeting with the evangelist during his upcoming trip to Belgium; and in Taipei, a Tokyo-based representative of the Billy Graham Evangelistic Association led a committee during a working lunch to plan a crusade there in the late fall.

Meanwhile, members of the Graham Team who had gathered in Jackson to assist with the activities of the crusade—formally known as the Greater Mississippi Crusade—began converging on the National Guard Armory. Billy would be arriving there soon to attend the 7th Annual Governor's Prayer Breakfast.

BREAKFAST AT THE ARMORY

It was the fourth day of the eight-day crusade. It was also the day that I had been invited to accompany Billy and his team through their hectic schedule. During the crusade's first few days, Billy had already held a press conference; sponsored a reception for local crusade leaders; addressed a ministers' meeting; attended the BGEA Team Breakfast, traditionally held on the opening day of every crusade; appeared on three television talk show programs; visited the offices of the advertising agency that was handling his public relations in Jackson; and toured the campus of a Presbyterian seminary that had recently dedicated a new building in memory of his late father-in-law, Dr. L. Nelson Bell.

At five minutes to eight, T.W. Wilson entered Billy's hotel room, handed him the morning newspaper, and announced that his brother, Grady, was downstairs waiting for them. "We've got to be out to the armory in fifteen minutes," T.W. said. Graham finished knotting a light blue tie, put on a maroon-colored sports jacket, and they headed out the door.

I was waiting for them in the lobby, which was crowded and noisy. It was filled with representatives of a local manufacturing firm that was conducting a sales conference in the hotel. As Graham stepped from the elevator, he was spotted quickly. An instant wave of excitement swept over the room—fingers pointed, arms stretched, and a sudden buzz of voices blotted out the hum of the lobby's piped-in music.

I followed T.W. as he skillfully propelled Billy through the crush of people and out the lobby door. Grady Wilson, who sat behind the wheel of a blue and white Pontiac sedan on North State Street, was waiting for us. Grady greeted us with that rich southern voice that was well known from the *Hour of Decision* radio program, on which he read from the Scriptures. Grady was never far from Billy's side during crusades, speaking engagements, or on foreign journeys. A great raconteur, he was always able to crack Billy up, especially with stories from the old days.

On the drive to the armory, as Billy went over his notes for his prayer breakfast talk, Grady reminisced about his own first sermon, which he preached at the Sixteenth Street Rescue Mission in their hometown of Charlotte, North Carolina. Grady's topic was "God's Four Questions," and he spent one-and-a-half hours on the first question. Grady said, "I can still see Billy and his date squirming, wondering if I'd ever finish. Well, I did," Grady said, "but by that time, everyone else was asleep!"

Although he had heard this story a thousand times before, Billy laughed at the memory. Then Grady talked about an incident that had taken place one day during the last Jackson Crusade, twenty-three years earlier. He and Cliff Barrows had gone on a fishing expedition and spent most of the time trading tall stories with some local ministers. When they returned, they found Billy in his room with a high fever and unable to speak. Grady recalled, "Billy looked at me and said, 'You've got to preach tonight.'" Grady then told us, "Well, I was tired and sunburned and had almost lost my voice, but I was not about to tell him that." The story was amusing as well as instructive; it gave me insight into how much more relaxed the Graham crusades had been twenty-odd years before. During this crusade, I would soon see that Cliff and Grady hardly had time to go out for a cup of coffee, let alone go fishing!

Billy turned to T.W. and asked about the day's schedule. T.W. handed Billy a typewritten sheet with the following information:

8:30	Governor's Prayer Breakfast
11:00	Address to School of Evangelism
12:00	Tour of Crusade Office
2:00	Staff Conferences
6:00	Departure for Stadium
7:30	Crusade Meeting
10:00	Dinner at Home of James Carr, Crusade Chairman

T.W. also reminded Billy that Johnny Cash and his wife, June Carter, were flying in later that day, and would be appearing at the evening meeting. Unfortunately, Johnny and June, who were close friends of Billy's, wouldn't be staying over. They had to return to Nashville immediately after the service to keep an early morning recording date.

Billy studied the schedule, which listed only his official functions and appointments; he knew that it showed only the basics,
and didn't accurately project what his day would really be like.
In fact, before the day was over, appointments and meetings
would be added; unplanned telephone calls would be made and
received; last-minute correspondence would require his attention;
and unexpected visitors would appear out of nowhere. In addition, during the afternoon, Billy would need to spend at least two
hours alone, going over the crusade's evening message, which
would be taped for national television distribution.

By the time we arrived at the National Guard Armory, it was
filled to capacity. Although we entered through a side door, as
soon as the charismatic Billy Graham walked into the huge hall,
he was noticed. A buzz permeated the armory, and all eyes were
focused on him. Governor Bill Waller, a kind of latter-day pop-
ulist, rose from his seat on the dais and walked over to greet Billy.
The governor, whose wife knew Grady Wilson since their school
days together in Charlotte, was genuinely pleased that the famed
evangelist was highlighting his prayer breakfast. When introducing Billy to the eager crowd, Governor Waller noted that Graham
represented those "Christian principles which many kinds of
people can agree upon." He continued:

> We have the honor of welcoming the world's greatest evan-
> gelist to Mississippi, and on behalf of 2.5 million God-fearing
> Mississippians, we welcome you to the Magnolia State, the
> friendliest state in the Union. We hope that your stay here will
> be one of the friendliest, warmest and, we hope, the most spir-
> itual visit that you've ever made to any part of the world.

In a thinly veiled reference to the racial issue, which had special pertinence in Jackson—long considered the last bastion of
opposition to legislative (and court-enforced) integration—Waller
called Graham "a symbol of the fact that people can get together
for worship without obstacles or barriers; he gives people a
chance to realize that with God there are no barriers."

At one point during the breakfast, Waller, who had had lunch with Billy at the executive mansion two days earlier, told me how impressed he was by the spiritual leader's grasp of current issues. The two had spent a congenial hour or so discussing politics. The governor also marveled at how relaxed Graham had appeared despite his heavy schedule. Waller told me that he and his wife " . . . support Billy with our money and our prayers." I believed him for two reasons: first, I wasn't a constituent he needed to impress; and second, because, constitutionally, he couldn't seek another term.

Among the subjects Graham broached when addressing the 1,850 breakfast guests was his concern that the credibility of the United States had been weakened by recent political events—in the immediate post-Watergate era, no one in the room had to ask what those events were. He maintained that this credibility gap had the whole world watching the United States, wondering if the nation would continue to live up to its commitments. In his closing words, Billy reminded the audience that it was nearly 1976—the year of the nation's bicentennial observance. He added that the commemoration must be launched on a "spiritual basis."

Billy stood on the dais as the crowd showed its appreciation with a standing ovation. Moments later, he was quickly ushered out of the armory and into the parking area, where Grady already had the Pontiac's engine running.

PLANNING THE JACKSON CRUSADE

By the time we left the armory, it was 9:30. Grady dropped us off at the hotel, and then headed for the School of Evangelism. He had to make sure the final arrangements for Billy's appearance there later that morning were in order. When we got back to the suite, Stephanie Wills was waiting there with a batch of letters for Billy. The mail, which came from the BGEA's Minneapolis headquarters, had been brought to Jackson the night before by Sherwood Wirt, then-editor of *Decision* magazine. "Woody," as he was affectionately known in the Graham organization, was in

Jackson to oversee the magazine's coverage of the crusade. Billy looked over the mail and separated out some letters that he wanted to answer during the next hour.

The phone rang, and Stephanie picked it up. It was Jim Carr, local chairman of the crusade's executive committee, calling to remind Billy of the dinner at his home later that evening. T.W. smiled and remarked that Carr was very persistent and persevering. When I asked what he meant, T.W. explained by telling me about the genesis of the Jackson Crusade.

About five years earlier, when Carr was president of the local Jaycees, his organization had passed a resolution, inviting Billy Graham to come to Jackson. Around the same time, a group of area ministers was also trying to influence Graham to hold a crusade there. The lay and clergy groups met and formed an *ad hoc* committee with Carr at its head. The committee's first order of business was to circulate a petition among the churches, asking Graham to come to its city.

Q. What do you like to read for relaxation?
A. *I have read most of the Louis L'Amour books. I like to read historical novels by authors like Antonia Fraser or someone like that. The one that made a great impression on me was* **Cromwell,** *which she wrote. I like to read books that have to do with medieval Europe and romances. I have read all of Sir Walter Scott's books, even Homer's* **Iliad.** *Before I was twenty, I had read the* **Book of Knowledge** *from one end to the other, and got my interest aroused in many different areas. I became interested in things my mother was interested in. For example, I've always wanted to see the Queen's Cathedral, or Mount Fujiyama because the* **Book of Knowledge** *had a picture of it.*

When Grady Wilson visited Jackson for an Easter sunrise service, he met with Carr. He explained that Billy would consider an invitation to the city only if it was broad-based and reflected the sentiment of the majority of the local churches. He advised

Carr that the invitation process was both detailed and demanding, and that there were also twenty cities in serious contention to host major crusades. In other words, it might be some time before Jackson could be put on the crusade schedule (if it was put on the schedule at all).

Carr, both a successful businessman and a devout believer, was determined to see the project through. He was also fortunate to have the support of his wife, Martha, who understood that her husband's efforts in developing a crusade would involve endless meetings, countless phone calls, and plenty of frustrations.

Several months after Wilson's visit to Jackson, Carr and four colleagues from the committee flew to Birmingham, Alabama, where Graham was conducting a crusade. On the afternoon of their arrival, they met with key Graham associates, including Grady Wilson and Cliff Barrows. Carr and his group brought along a book that was filled with letters from state and city officials and local civic and religious leaders, supporting the appearance of a Billy Graham Crusade in Jackson. They also presented detailed information provided by the city's Chamber of Commerce on Jackson's economic and social structure, as well as the facilities that would be available to accommodate the crusade.

Grady and Cliff were impressed enough to ask the delegation, which was ready to catch a plane back home that afternoon, to stay overnight to meet with Graham. And later that evening, just prior to the service, Carr and his group were able to spend a few moments with the evangelist, who promised that the city of Jackson would be given careful consideration.

Most of the committee members returned to Jackson, expecting that a crusade would be held in their city within the year. Carr, however, knew that they were only at the beginning of the process. And for the next two years, he kept the committee alive, never allowing himself the option of becoming discouraged. Later, however, he did acknowledge that there were many times when he doubted that a crusade would ever take place in Jackson.

During that period, Carr's committee stayed in touch with

Walter Smyth, who was head of crusade scheduling for the Graham organization. Smyth continually told the group that Jackson was on the list, but there was no definite commitment yet. In the fall of 1974, Sterling Huston, who was put in charge of Graham's North American schedule, came to Jackson. He met with Carr's committee, as well as a larger group of local leadership. Two months later, almost four years after the original Jaycee resolution had been passed, Sterling telephoned Jim Carr with the good news—Mr. Graham wanted to come to Jackson in May of 1975.

At that point, the *ad hoc* committee was formalized into the official crusade committee and Carr was elected chairperson. The Graham organization, which relied heavily on local participation for a maximally effective crusade, preferred to have a lay person head this committee. In the words of Sterling Huston, the committee chairperson needed to be "a successful businessman who was used to getting the job done." Carr, whose dogged determination was, at that point, a matter of record, certainly fit the bill.

Along with Carr, the crusade committee appointed three ministers as vice-chairpersons, who represented the community's major denominations—Baptist, Methodist, and Presbyterian. They, along with twenty other individuals comprised the executive committee. This group was divided into subcommittees that were responsible for various facets of the crusade, such as organizing prayer groups, youth activities, fundraisers, counselors, women's groups, ushers, and follow-up teams.

The executive committee was also responsible for drawing up a budget for the crusade. Crusade budgets, which were always based on actual costs, differed from city to city. Typically, their most significant single cost was for the auditorium or stadium rental. In some places, these sites were free; in others, rental costs were quite steep. For example, the local committee for the 1969 New York Crusade paid $22,000 per evening for the use of Madison Square Garden. In Jackson, the 46,000-seat football stadium was available for a relatively nominal cost.

Crusade Budget

The budget for the Jackson Crusade was eventually fixed at
$266,000. This money was raised in several ways. First, the
finance committee worked closely with the Graham organization
to develop a group of "Share Partners" who donated money for
the crusade's operation. These people, whose names came from
the *Decision* magazine mailing list, lived within a fifty-mile radius
of Jackson; they received letters from the BGEA asking for help as
Share Partners. Typically, the funds raised from Share Partners
paid the pre-crusade costs. For the Jackson Crusade, there were
approximately 2,000 participants. To raise additional money,
committee members also conducted individual solicitations,
which accounted for a third of the budget costs. The remainder of
the money came from offerings that were collected at each crusade session.

Committee Work

Once the administrative committee was organized and the
budget fixed, the BGEA sent in a specialist to serve both as the
director of the entire crusade operation and as a liaison between
the association and the local sponsoring committee. The local
committee made all of the decisions involving the crusade's conduct, while the crusade director was responsible for the execution
of those decisions.

The Jackson group was fortunate to have the services of
Charles Riggs, an organizing genius of the first rank and seasoned veteran of countless big-city crusades. As Jim Carr said,
"When I heard that Charlie Riggs was being assigned to Jackson,
I knew everything was going to be all right." A tall, raw-boned,
graying native of Texas, Riggs had been with Graham since 1953.
Before then, he had worked with the Navigators, an evangelistic
group that carried on an aggressive Scripture memorization ministry among the armed services.

In January 1975, Charlie and his wife left their Nashville
home and took an apartment in Jackson, which would be their

temporary home until the crusade was over. An office with about 3,000 square feet of working space, located adjacent to the stadium, was rented, and became the hub of crusade activity for the next four months. A paid staff of ten was assembled, including a bookkeeper, secretaries, and skilled mailing clerks. And hundreds of volunteers were recruited to stuff envelopes, prepare mailers, and perform the many nuts-and-bolts chores involved in putting together a crusade.

Under Riggs's direction, metropolitan Jackson was broken down into ten geographic areas. Each area, led by a designated chairman, was broken down into groups of men, women, youth, and pastors, providing the crusade with four lines into the local churches. Each area chairman completed a three-week Bible study course and received a thorough orientation in the various aspects of the crusade operation. Each chairman also identified and trained two additional echelons of workers—one representing areas as defined by zip codes, and the other representing a specific area's churches. The workers were then channeled into a prayer program in which 60,000 local residents would eventually become involved. These participants met daily to pray for the crusade's success.

Once the prayer groups were set in motion, Riggs met with the pastors in each area. He shared the crusade plans, and also encouraged them to recruit their congregants to volunteer as counselors, ushers, and choir members. The pastors were also urged to bring busloads of people to the crusade sessions—an aspect of the effort known as "Operation Andrew." In the 1971 Dallas-Fort Worth Crusade, Operation Andrew brought in nearly 40,000 people to each session. In Jackson, it would account for an average of 22,000 reservations per evening—a significant attendance base when trying to fill a 46,000-seat stadium.

The various committees' intensive organizing efforts mobilized a significant portion of the church community to get involved with the crusade. Reflecting on the impact of this involvement, Jim Carr remarked, "Even if for some reason the Graham people had at the last minute to cancel out, it would have been worth it. People joined together in Bible study, prayer, and got to know each other."

SPREADING THE WORD

Four weeks before the first day of the crusade, Cliff Barrows flew into Jackson for a workers' rally at the Calvary Baptist Church. At about the same time, a special men's breakfast was held in the First Baptist Church; Tom Landry, the coach of the Dallas Cowboys, was the featured speaker.

Up to that point, most of the organizational activity had been internal in nature. Once all of the workers were identified, trained, and fired with enthusiasm, the crusade committee turned its attention to the general public. Through advertisements on billboards and buses, in newspapers, and on radio programs, the residents of Jackson, Mississippi, learned that Billy Graham was coming to town soon. There was an air of excitement in Jackson. And by the time I arrived, four days before the crusade began, "Billy Graham" seemed to be the name on everybody's lips.

5

The Morning
Continues

BACK AT THE HOLIDAY INN, GRAHAM was in the middle of dictating a note to Stephanie Wills when Cliff Barrows walked into the room. One of the original team members, Cliff, with his wife, Billie, traveled with Billy, Grady, and George Beverly Shea in the early post-World War II days. Thirty years of close association with Graham had not dulled his appreciation and respect for the man at all.

Although Cliff was best known as the crusade musical director and emcee, he also served as Graham's radio and television program director. Each service was taped for possible television usage. Cliff studied the film and determined how much of the material could be processed for national distribution. Cliff was smiling as he walked into the room. He told Billy that the TV tape of the previous evening's service looked very good and required little editing. Cliff was also responsible for the *Hour of Decision* radio broadcast. This vital job, along with his recording dates and personal appearance schedule, kept him very busy.

An ordained Baptist minister and an outstanding speaker, Cliff served as an assistant pastor of St. Paul's Temple Baptist Church in Minnesota back in the mid-forties. He would have been satisfied to pursue a career in the ministry, but believed that he was called by God to work with Graham. Indeed, his relationship with the evangelist gave Barrows a far greater opportunity to preach to larger and more diverse audiences than he ever could have hoped for as the pastor of a local congregation.

After delivering the good news about the previous evening's

film, Cliff told Billy that he was leaving for the School of Evangelism and would see him there later. As I was interested in viewing Billy through Cliff's eyes, I asked if I could ride along with him to the school, which convened at the First Baptist Church.

During the drive, I asked Cliff how he accounted for Billy's success. "His simplicity, sincerity, and integrity are the three primary reasons for his success," he responded. "This is why God has opened so many doors for him. You have to remember that Billy has an absolute trust in the word of God. He has been a man of integrity and consistency in the proclamation of God's message." Barrows spoke also of Graham's unique gifts. He recalled that even in the early days, Billy had a keen interest in political affairs.

I ask Cliff what it was like to be with Billy for long periods of time. Was he temperamental? How did he treat his staff and associates? Cliff replied, "I've spent as much time with him as I have with my family—in a sense, the team is a family—and after thirty years, he is as warm and friendly and as interested in people as he ever was. Many men along in years are content with what they have accomplished. I'm continually amazed at his interest in every aspect of the Kingdom of God."

I was interested in what Barrows said about being with Graham as much as he was with his own wife and children—didn't this cause a strain in the family's relations? But like all the other key people around Graham, Cliff was convinced that he was part of a vital, even historic, ministry. Thus he and his associates were able to make personal sacrifices that others, working in more mundane circumstances, would not consider. He told me that even when his children were very little, they understood that "Daddy has to be away with Billy Graham." One evening, however, his eight-year-old son prayed, "God, save everybody so Daddy can stay home."

SCHOOL OF EVANGELISM

When we reached the First Baptist Church, I was handed a packet of materials describing the School of Evangelism and its program. The initial paragraphs of welcome read:

> The Billy Graham School of Evangelism is designed to focus your attention on the dynamic of the Gospel. This supplement to seminary studies is designed to inspire pastors and key lay leaders to a greater emphasis on evangelistic activity together with tested methods for local church outreach. In this crisis hour of our nation's history, the church is confronted with its greatest opportunity. The School is planned to enable the pastor to take maximum advantage of the times in which we live.
>
> We are here to enjoy five days of intellectually and spiritually exciting moments. Make new friends. Mutually share spiritual experiences. Discuss programs which are working in the field of evangelism. Be available to God. There are menial and exalted opportunities awaiting you. Be early to each meeting. Don't miss a word of an event. To this unique experience Billy Graham and his entire Team welcome you.

Later I learned more about the school and its mode of operation from the dean, Dr. Kenneth Chafin, who, along with Harold Lindsell, editor of *Christianity Today;* Sherwood Wirt, editor of *Decision* magazine; and Dr. Robert D. Ferm, represented the intellectual vanguard of the Graham movement.

Chafin had a distinguished academic and organizational background. He was the Billy Graham Professor of Evangelism at Southern Baptist Theological Seminary and head of the Department of Evangelism of the Southern Baptist Convention. He was also the author of several books, host of the syndicated television series *Spring Street U.S.A.,* and pastor of Houston's South Main Baptist Church, one of the largest congregations in the United States.

Chafin described the history of the School of Evangelism in didactic yet enthusiastic terms. The school owed its formation to Lowell Berry, a Presbyterian layman from San Francisco who served on the board of a Bay Area seminary and was active in the 1971 Oakland Crusade. He came away from the crusade convinced that theological students were not being exposed to the evangelistic orientation manifested by Graham. So he asked Billy to set up a school of evangelism for theological students in conjunction with the crusades. Although Billy liked the idea, he had many other matters on his mind when Berry first made the proposal. Berry, however, was quite persistent. And, finally, after Graham said, "Well, Lowell, this is going to cost a lot of money," Berry replied that he was prepared to provide the necessary funding.

Q. Will the Internet and new advances in communication change the nature and techniques of evangelism?

A. *It is amazing how technology is being used to hurt the world. But it is also being used to spread the Gospel on a scale that has never happened in the history of the Christian Church. It is a time for the church to utilize this technology to make a worldwide statement that in the midst of chaos, emptiness, and despair, there is hope in the person of Jesus Christ. We, too, need to explore every legitimate method for reaching our world for Christ. New challenges call for new methods and new strategies. I like to use modern technology. I think this technology, which can be used for evil or good, is being used by us to present the Gospel to the whole world.*

While this school was able to operate in various settings, Chafin maintained that the "atmosphere of the crusade created an unbelievable context for learning." At first, the student body consisted only of seminarians, but pastors were later included, and, finally, lay people were also invited to participate. School sessions, with their annual budget exceeding $250,000, were held at each crusade. The students' lodging was paid for by the Graham organization, and they also received a stipend to help defray the cost of transportation.

As the Jackson Crusade was regional in nature, the school drew pupils not only from Mississippi, but also from Alabama, Tennessee, and Louisiana. Sessions were held Monday through Friday and consisted of a daily morning plenary, six or seven afternoon seminars, and attendance at each evening's crusade service. During the week, the school's 1,300 registrants would hear from Grady Wilson, Harold Lindsell, Charles Riggs, and other team members. They would also hear from Dr. Basil Jackson, a clinical psychiatrist on the faculty of the University of Wisconsin; Dr. Paul Little, author and assistant to the president of the Inter-Varsity Christian Fellowship; and Dr. Charles L. Allen, pastor of the 11,000-member First United Methodist Church of Houston.

I posed a few questions to Chafin: Why did Graham bother to come to Jackson, a medium-sized city with a huge number of churches and, presumably, a very high density of evangelical Christians? Wasn't it an easy ride for Graham? Shouldn't he be trying to reach the tougher northern cities with their large "un-churched" populations?

Chafin, while soft-spoken, was very direct and unapologetic. He explained the strategy in going to smaller cities. Jackson, like Albuquerque, New Mexico (the first stop on Graham's 1975 itinerary), and Lubbock, Texas (the next port of call), needed less preparation than that required by crusades held in major metropolitan areas. Crusades in smaller cities could also be televised and aired throughout the United States. Thus, by conducting crusades in the Jacksons and the Lubbocks, Graham had more opportunities for coverage than he did by holding fewer, and, by necessity, longer crusades in big cities.

"Why then," I asked, "go to the trouble of coming to Jackson at all? Why not just produce a program in a television studio?" Chafin explained that you can never get the same effect and excitement in a studio. But more important, Graham's appearances in places like Albuquerque, Jackson, and Lubbock revitalized and energized the local churches and provided vehicles for cooperation and united action that had a long-lasting, positive impact.

Chafin's words brought to mind a conversation I had with Jim Carr, who spoke of the "lifetime effect the crusade had upon my life," adding that the crusade "made me realize what it means to be a Christian; it made me understand that though we live in the Bible Belt, we still have a mission in our neighborhood."

"Anyway," Chafin concluded, "Billy does go to some very difficult places, like Seoul, Korea, where he pulled over 1 million people to a service, and Baltimore, where he will hold a major crusade in 1976."

I then asked Chafin the question I posed to many of Graham's associates during my stay in Jackson: Why is Graham so successful whether he is standing on evangelical turf or on relatively alien ground? Chafin responded by saying that to answer that question fully, one must seek to understand the success of evangelical Christianity itself. He said:

> The emptiness of man and the adequacy of the Gospel transcend the Moodys and the Billy Grahams. The Gospel is unchanging and has survived as something much more attractive than the various alternatives which have caught the public's attention. I feel evangelicalism is just at the beginning of its best period in recent history. Liberal Christianity has pretty much struck out and evangelical Christianity has become a little more whole, more interested in a ministry to the total person.

As Cliff and I walked through the halls of the First Baptist Church, the morning's plenary for the School of Evangelism broke for a fifteen-minute recess. When it resumed, Graham was scheduled to speak. The sanctuary doors opened and the students began to flow into the hallway; I had the opportunity to speak with several of them. One, a thirty-year-old pastor from a rural Mississippi town, told me how delighted he was to be there. He said, "This is like a blood transfusion to me; you really can stagnate when you're out there away from the seminary, theological libraries, and interaction with colleagues."

I wondered how effectively Graham would be able to communicate with this young man, as well as with the other pastors and church workers who had come to Jackson from dozens of southern hamlets and way-stops. Could he possibly understand their problems and concerns? Was he aware of the lives they led, the issues that were important in their delta outposts? While it's true that Graham had grown up on a farm—the Charlotte of his youth was a relatively small town, sheltered from the glitter and sophisticated façade of the large population centers—he had come a long way from that Charlotte homestead. He was now preoccupied with the enormous challenges entailed in running a worldwide operation.

I also wondered if his fame intimidated his audiences. Or if there would be a current of jealousy, even among the ministers of the Jackson churches. Wouldn't some ask themselves why Graham had risen so far while they labored in the provinces? Of course, ideally, all Christian workers were expected to be happy within the context of their lives, because each person's role was part of God's plan. Furthermore, God couldn't utilize too many Billy Grahams; after all, there had to be foot soldiers to carry out the routine tasks that were important in building the Kingdom of God.

BILLY ADDRESSES THE STUDENTS

With their break over, the students excitedly reassembled in anticipation of their guest speaker. After a gracious introduction from Chafin and a standing ovation, Billy, who looked very relaxed and confident as he stood in the pulpit, began to speak. It didn't take long before my question regarding Graham's ability to relate to this audience was answered—he could and he did.

Graham, who was always on the lookout for jokes or anecdotes to use in his messages, began his speech to the students by telling them that he had hoped to play some golf while in Jackson. Unfortunately, the weather was not cooperating. He said that a couple days earlier, a rainstorm had forced him and some members of the crusade committee off a course after only five holes. He also mentioned that Grady had not been with him on the course that day. Instead, Grady was following the advice Sam Snead had once given him—stop playing for two or three months . . . and then give up the game completely! The audience chuckled in appreciation.

Billy then spoke of the man whose wife was after him because he wasn't going to Sunday school. She said, "You know, there are three reasons why you should be in Sunday school every Sunday. One is that you had a godly mother who always insisted you go to Sunday school, and she'd be disappointed if you didn't go. The second reason is you're now over forty years old, and it's time you established good habits. And third, you're pastor of the church!"

This last story broke the audience up; but when the laughter died down, Graham became serious. His comments reflected the changes he had seen in Jackson since his last crusade there:

> I commend you for the way you have reacted to the tremendous social changes which have taken place in this state since we were here twenty-three years ago. Many people wondered why we came to Jackson when we could go to this city or that city that's larger than Jackson. I answered by saying that we came here to get something of the blessing and the thrill and the joy that we find here in Mississippi among both black and white people that I believe has made a contribution to our own team, that's opened the eyes of some of our own team members about Mississippi. And I also wanted to say something on the television about Mississippi to the people in other parts of the country, which I am able to do.

As I heard these words, I was tempted to think that Graham was pandering to his audience. Yet I knew from our conversations that he really believed that the South, and even the Deep South, had advanced dramatically in terms of racial accord. As a southerner, Graham often felt a sense of frustration, even outrage, when charges were made of the South's recalcitrance on the racial issue. Graham's reaction was, to some degree, similar to the feelings expressed by his very close friend, former President Lyndon Johnson, on hearing the South maligned because of its racial problems.

W.F. Minor, the Mississippi correspondent of the New Orleans *Times-Picayune*, discussed this theme in a dispatch from Jackson:

> When the idea of getting Graham back came up in local

church circles nearly two years ago, it was learned that the evangelist would not deal with any group unless it had a totally biracial structure. This set in motion what some church leaders now are saying is a healthy new basis for interracial communication, which has been slow to come in certain church circles here.

On Cooperative Evangelism

Billy then told his audience that despite what he had heard concerning the economic problems of Mississippi, he was impressed with the size of the crusade offerings. "Either you love the Lord far more than any other place we have ever been and you give, or you may not be tithing to your church and you give it to us," he said, drawing another wave of laughter and applause.

When the audience settled down, Graham talked of the fellowship he has enjoyed with people representing many denominations. "You know," he said, "after a while you begin to see that God has his people everywhere."

As his ministry broadened, Graham was criticized by evangelicalism's right wing for consorting with mainline denominational types and "liberals." One could only wonder what the reaction of these folks would be if Billy accepted his recent invitation to hold a crusade on the campus of Notre Dame University.

Years ago, Graham's philosophy of inclusionism, as it related to crusade sponsorship, was outlined in a book entitled *Cooperative Evangelism*. Graham felt that evangelicals tended to be too exclusive in their outreach, thus limiting the scope and potential impact of their ministry. He has made a concerted effort to bring to a crusade as wide a scope of community support as possible, albeit within the context of a basic commitment to the doctrine of personal salvation through Christ.

In a place as heavily saturated with evangelicals as Jackson, most of the churches that refused to cooperate with the crusade represented an extreme right-wing viewpoint. The situation would have been very different in cities like Boston, Chicago, and New York, where opposition to Graham's ministry normally came from the more liberally oriented congregations. Despite the problems emanating from the poles of American Protestantism, a typical Graham crusade won the support of about 80 percent of the local churches. That, along with encouragement engendered by civic groups, provided a very firm base for a successful operation. An editorial in the *Baptist Record,* the official journal of the Mississippi Baptist Convention, dealt with this question of cooperation:

> As to compromise, if there has been any, it is that the liberals and non-evangelicals have compromised their position in cooperating with Billy Graham. Not for one moment has he ever compromised his position that the Bible is the inspired Word of God, or that every person is a sinner and must be born again through repentance between God and faith in the Lord Jesus Christ.

Next, Graham mentioned that he and some associates, including Charlie Riggs, had recently been in Northeast India, where they preached to audiences representing seven language groups. "They told me there would be a sunrise service, and I said, 'Oh, let Charlie take it;' then they said there will be 100,000 people there, and I said, 'I think I'll take it!'"

The Sermon

Before he began his actual sermon, Graham thanked Ken Chafin for his leadership and for being "a pastor to pastors." He also commended Dr. Pollard, the pastor of the First Baptist Church, for lending the excellent facilities, and he mentioned Lowell Berry, who came to each crusade to observe the operation of the School of Evangelism.

The transition to the message was rather abrupt. Graham opened his Bible and said, "I want to take a text that all of you have preached on many, many times, I Corinthians 1:17–18:

> . . . for Christ sent me not to baptize but to preach the Gospel,

not with wisdom of words, lest the cross of Christ be made of none effect, for the preaching of the cross is to them as foolishness, but unto us which are saved it is the power of God.

The theme of Graham's sermon revolved around the problem of making the Gospel relevant to modern man. He told the pastors and church workers sitting before him that they should expect their listeners to have emptiness, loneliness, guilt, the fear of death, and a deep-seated insecurity "in their hearts."

To be effective, the Gospel must be preached as a holy word with authority, simplicity, repetition, and urgency. "It's not your logic or intellectualism or your arguments, and it's not mine which work," Graham cautioned his audience. "There is something about the Gospel that has its own power."

Billy's comments did not suggest that he was anti-intellectual or irrational in his approach. He believed that the Bible had supernatural powers, and he fully expected people to respond to his message if he was faithful in articulating the teaching of the Scriptures. His sermons were replete with Biblical references; perhaps their most common shared phrase was "The Bible says." When he told his audience that the Gospel "has its own power," he was not speaking only in theory, but also of many years of personal experience and observation.

As an evangelist, Billy understood that his particular calling was to inform men of their sinfulness and of their need to accept Jesus as Lord and Savior. His work was to bring men to the point where, in total submission to God, they recognized their utter dependence on Christ's work of redemption at the cross, and allowed Jesus to come into their lives to bring them salvation.

He constantly repeated classic scriptural passages that summarized the process of salvation. Among them, he often quoted John 3:16: "For God so loved the world, He gave His only begotten Son, that whosoever believeth in Him shall not perish but shall have everlasting life," and Romans 10:9: "If thou shalt confess with thy mouth the Lord Jesus and believe in thine heart that God hath raised Him from the dead, thou shalt be saved."

Once salvation has been accomplished, the sinner becomes transformed: he is a new person; he receives a new nature and a new heart. One of Graham's favorite and most often quoted verses of Scripture, II Corinthians 5:17, describes this new birth: "If any man be in Christ he is a new person, old things are put away, all things become new." The way has been paved for a person to take on the godly traits of love, joy, long-suffering, and patience, and to put aside intolerance and bigotry. The new man in Christ is better equipped than the most ardent social reformer or religious do-gooder to bring about long-term, decisive, and positive changes in the social structure.

This concept had great potential pertinence in a place like Jackson, Mississippi, where manifestations of the new life in Christ were sadly lacking in relations between the races. And while Graham's first order of business—here as elsewhere in the world—was to bring men to acceptance of Christ, the impact of his visit to Jackson would also be evaluated in terms of modifications or changes in personal and corporate racial attitudes resulting from his ministry.

TRIP TO THE CRUSADE OFFICE

Shortly after the conclusion of the sermon, Grady, Billy, and I piled into the car and headed to our next stop—the crusade office. Grady drove up North State Street to Woodrow Wilson Avenue, made a left, and pulled in front of the American Public Life Building. We walked up to the second floor, and as Billy entered the office, he was greeted by about fifty workers who stared at him in open-mouthed surprise. Save for the incessant ringing of the many telephones scattered about the room, everything came to a stop as Billy approached each person with words of greeting and appreciation. This action was no mechanical exercise suggested by a Madison Avenue brain. Although Billy had never seen these workers before, nor was he likely to ever see them again, his interest in meeting them was genuine.

There was no particular need to visit the headquarters—

indeed, the time could have been better spent resting or preparing for the next day's meeting with his executive board. Among the many items on the agenda for that all-day meeting were a number of urgent, schedule-related matters that needed to be settled. Nevertheless, Graham patiently signed autographs and exchanged pleasantries with these people, who had worked so hard to ensure a successful crusade. Billy then sat for a few minutes in Charlie Riggs' office, where he was briefed on platform arrangements for Johnny Cash's visit later that night.

One of the workers, teenager Joyce Gomez, approached Graham and told him about her friend who had come to Christ at the service the evening before. Joyce had been praying for this girl, was thrilled at her conversion, and wanted to share the good news with Billy. He asked Joyce for her friend's name, and then instructed Charlie Riggs to make sure that there was adequate follow-up.

It was, of course, impossible for Graham to keep track of all of his converts; this follow-up was primarily the job of the local committee and churches, who had to insure that each of those individuals was put in contact with a local congregation. Normally, within forty-eight hours after a person comes forward at a crusade service, a counselor reaches him or her via telephone, mail, or a personal visit. Graham was, however, greatly interested in learning about individual conversions, and his mail reflected the variety of those who came to Christ as the result of his ministry.

Graham was often criticized for not remaining in a community to personally oversee the follow-up once a crusade had ended. Not only was this logistically impossible, it ran counter to Billy's perception of his evangelistic role. He believed that the Christian ministry called for a division of activities, and that it was the role of others to nurture the new converts, transforming them into mature believers. Billy saw his role as the catalyst—the agent used by God to bring a person who has been moved by the Holy Spirit to make a decision for Christ. This was Billy's particular gift, and even his severest critics had to acknowledge that he always remained consistently faithful to his calling.

Unlike many other evangelists, who came into a town, won souls, and then left without establishing a mechanism for follow-up, the Graham organization provided the training and materials that enabled local Christians to conduct successful follow-up campaigns. In addition to being put in touch with a local church within a day or two after committing their lives to Christ, new converts were contacted again about three weeks after the crusade to determine if they were attending those churches. Each inquirer also received *Decision* magazine as well as periodic letters from Graham for one year following the crusade. When inquirers came forward during a meeting, they were given a booklet containing a correspondence course on the relationship with Christ. The local committee also sponsored a radio Bible-study program that aired twice a day; this helped maintain the atmosphere of the crusade until the churches were able to assign the major work of follow-up.

It is at this point that so many of Graham's critics err when they present "studies"—more often theories—to prove that Graham's converts do not last. In fact, maintaining the long-term commitment of a Graham-crusade convert is not the responsibility of the Graham organization. Local churches and Christians have a much greater responsibility in lending outreach and continued support to newly converted individuals.

It is also true that, despite claims to the contrary, a great percentage of Graham converts do remain within the evangelical fold. Many become active, highly motivated believers. One has only to talk with a cross section of seminarians at evangelical schools or visit local congregations around the United States to gauge the tremendous impact of Graham's ministry.

Many of Graham's critics are also shortsighted in that they fail to note his impact upon the public at large. Invariably, Billy Graham is the first name that comes to mind when one is asked to identify America's most important religious leader. His position on values-oriented concerns, such as the right to life, pornography, and family relationships, as well as issues of social justice, including race relations, religious bias, poverty, hunger, and public morality, are of tremendous, and, I believe, increasing influence.

MORE THAN A PREACHER

Several years earlier, a major politician said of Graham, "He is more than a preacher, more than an evangelist, more than a Christian leader. In a greater sense, he has become our conscience." While this statement may be going too far, in a period when the pantheon of political and public leaders has been sorely depleted, Graham remains one of the few remaining authoritative and respected national personalities.

Unlike many instant celebrities, he is not a creation of the media. And although he has acknowledged the importance of the Hearst newspapers' coverage of his first Los Angeles Crusade in 1949, his great prestige has been built on a solid base of achievement over a period of decades.

Two presidents have wanted Graham to serve in their cabinets, and he could have had his pick of diplomatic or ceremonial posts. Graham, however, resisted all of these tempting offers, not only because he viewed himself as serving a higher power, but also because he realized that identification with a particular political party or acceptance of a specific governmental responsibility would diminish his spiritual effectiveness and, ultimately, weaken his organization and power base.

There are, of course, ordained clergy in the Congress. And at least two ministers have worked in the White House: Bill Moyers, an ordained Southern Baptist in the Johnson administration; and Father John McLaughlin, a Jesuit priest, in the Nixon presidency. None of these individuals, however, has enjoyed the opportunities for direct Christian service that confront and challenge Billy Graham.

The playing field of the stadium fills with people as they accept Billy's invitation.

6

Noon

IT WAS 12:30 BY THE TIME WE LEFT the School of Evangelism, and Charlie Riggs suggested that we stop for a bite to eat before returning to the Holiday Inn. Billy said, "Fine, let's go someplace nearby." We drove over to Morrison's Cafeteria, a popular inexpensive restaurant located near the Mississippi Memorial Stadium.

It was almost impossible for Billy to have a meal in a restaurant without people continually coming over to his table to talk to him or to get his autograph. The experience at Morrison's was typical. Billy was wearing a golf cap and dark glasses in an effort to avoid drawing attention to himself, but as he made his way through the line, a murmur went up from behind the serving counter. And no sooner was the soup placed on his tray, when people begin to shout, "There's Billy Graham!"

We sat down in a booth and people began to converge on Billy immediately. Grady and Charlie, who had already put in a good day's work, were hungry and quickly demolished their sandwiches. But the besieged Billy managed to down only a couple spoonfuls of chicken soup and a few forkfuls of salad.

One elderly lady was especially persistent in demanding Billy's attention. She wanted his picture, but, unfortunately, no one nearby had a camera. So she insisted that he mail her one, adding, "And be sure it's autographed!" Graham responded with the unfailing good grace and patience of one who has spent years in countless eateries, listening to similar requests. Grady jotted the woman's name and address in a small binder notebook.

"I think it's time to go," Grady said. But Billy was busy shaking hands with people at adjoining tables. He told a teenage couple, who had interrupted their admiration for each other to turn their attention to him, "Be sure to come out tonight. Johnny Cash will be singing, and I'm going to preach on the problems of young people." As an added incentive in getting them to attend the crusade, he turned to Charlie Riggs and said, "Charlie, give these folks a pass to the reserved section. I know they're going to enjoy the service." Then Billy was out the door and standing by the car, waiting for the rest of us to catch up.

Back in the car, I asked Billy if he was bothered by his celebrity status—that he couldn't go out to eat, shop, or engage in other everyday activities without being stared at and interrupted. Billy was rather philosophical about this problem, which he knew would never go away. His only concern was that he always remained courteous and Christlike in his response. He explained:

I have been placed by God in a particular situation. There are great pressures, but also great rewards. The people who come up to me and want to meet and talk to me normally do so from a legitimate motivation. I feel I should respond to them. Of course, it is impossible to see everyone, and listen to their concerns. Why in Jackson alone, I have received 275 requests for private interviews and appointments. Obviously, I cannot see but a small fraction of these people. I find I have to consider prayerfully who I should see and how I should most effectively use my time. In my mind at all times is the desire to glorify God in my actions and be as fruitful as is humanly possible in His service.

I asked Billy if he worried about being physically attacked when he was approached by people in public places. He replied that there was always the danger that a crazed person would attempt to harm him. Years earlier in San Diego, he had had a close call when a man came at him with a knife.

Although two or three plainclothes detectives protected Billy during crusades, he was an easy target for attack when preaching in huge open-air stadiums. He admitted that there was little he could do to protect himself. His attitude reminded me of President John F. Kennedy's. On the morning of his assassination, Kennedy pointed to a building and reportedly said, "A nut could easily shoot me from a rooftop." As one who believes he has been called to reach as many men as possible for Christ, Graham cannot live in a shelter; he cannot hide his candle, or even his body, under a bushel. He must go out into the world and preach the Gospel, no matter the personal danger.

Later, when I heard that Billy had received an invitation to hold a crusade in a country that had experienced a number of political assassinations, I was concerned for his safety. I expressed that fear to T.W., who nodded and candidly responded, saying that he feared for his own safety as well. "After all," he observed, "I'm the guy who will be standing next to Billy."

AN URGENT REQUEST

Back at the hotel, several urgent telephone messages awaited Billy's attention—the most pressing came from the island of Guam. There, thousands of Vietnamese refugees had been taken on the first stop in the flight from their native land. Billy was very concerned with the plight of these people. Although he had been severely criticized in the past for not speaking out on the war in Indochina, the evangelist had been keenly interested in events in Southeast Asia, particularly the problem of human suffering that resulted from the bitter fighting there.

Graham first became familiar with the unrest in that part of the world in 1962 during a visit with President Kennedy. He continued to be fully informed on the progress of the war by his close friend President Johnson, and then by President Nixon. Beginning in the mid-1960s, liberal Christians put Graham under great pressure to speak out on the war; but he felt that doing so would be indiscreet. He did, however, go to Vietnam several times to minister to the troops. On one occasion, his visit coincided with a special mission undertaken by the militantly pro-war Francis Cardinal Spellman of New York. Newsmen tried to get Graham to agree with Spellman's strongly favorable statements on U.S. policy, but Billy wisely demurred. Unfortunately, because the two religious leaders happened to be in Vietnam at the same time, some people were led to believe that their views were similar, and Graham was labeled a "hawk."

> **Q.** Do you root for any specific sports teams?
>
> **A.** *I have followed the Atlanta Braves quite a bit. That's the closest franchise to us. In football, the Carolina Panthers are my team. I've always pulled for the New York Yankees ever since I had the privilege of shaking hands with Babe Ruth when I was a boy.*

On the other hand, Graham was genuinely worried about the possibility of a Communist takeover in Southeast Asia, and there was little question that he supported American foreign policy during most of the 1960s. The many rallies, demonstrations, and other antiwar incidents notwithstanding, he joined millions of other Americans in taking that position.

Several of Billy's critics suggested that he was involved in policymaking during the Vietnam conflict. But that simply was not true. Although he was informed by President Nixon of the incursion into Cambodia several hours before that operation was launched, he had no voice in the decision to broaden the war's scope, nor did he have any input regarding other controversial aspects of America's involvement, such as the bombing of Hanoi. Graham did, however, attempt to articulate the concerns of evangelicals regarding the fate of the Christian missionaries who had remained in Indochina long after the fighting had begun.

Meanwhile, the pressing call at the Holiday Inn from Guam was from refugee officials, who urged Graham to suspend his current schedule and fly there immediately. They believed he would be able to bring a message of comfort and hope to the many Vietnamese people who were stunned and disoriented by the rapid change in their lives. Graham was sorely tempted to say yes, but he recognized the importance of his presence at the Jackson Crusade. He would not ask his associates to assume responsibility for the meetings while he went off to Guam.

There was no sense of pride or arrogance at play in his decision—it was a matter of honoring his commitment to the people of Jackson. Through many years of crusade experience, he knew that people were coming out to see and hear Billy Graham. The entire effort, which had been nearly five years in the making, was built around *him*. And although there were a number of competent preachers who could have filled in if Billy were to leave, he knew that the crusade would lose its focus, its *raison d'être*.

Yet Graham could not summarily reject the refugee officials' request. If possible, he wanted to make the trip to Guam immediately following the crusade. The biggest obstacle, however, was that he had to be back in Charlotte two days later, where he was being honored as "Man of the South." Although this accolade was relatively unimportant to Billy on a personal level, President Ford was coming in for the event, so he couldn't cancel.

Billy tried to arrange his schedule to accommodate the trip. If he left for Guam immediately after the crusade ended on Sunday, could he get back to Charlotte by Tuesday? Grady got right to work. He checked flight schedules, while taking into consideration such matters as flying time, time differences between the countries, and the number of hours it would take to meet and speak with the refugees. Unfortunately, the trip turned out to be an impossibility. A disappointed Billy called the U.S. representative on Guam, and regrettably informed him of the logistical problems entailed in making the trip. However, in an attempt to help the island's Christian leaders and officials in supporting the refugees, Billy and Grady spent a considerable amount of time on the phone that afternoon and during the following days, offering guidance and suggestions.

DR. E.V. HILL

It was nearly 1:15, and Graham had several appointments scheduled. He asked T.W. to take care of some phone calls for him, and then directed his secretary to hold all others until further notice.

There was a knock on the outer door, and Dr. E.V. Hill, pastor of the Mount Zion Baptist Church in South Central Los Angeles, walked into the room. Dr. Hill was the first black member to serve on the board of the BGEA. A massive man, he greeted Billy with a huge bear hug.

"Ed, how have you been? How are things in Watts?" Billy asked.

"I'm just great, Billy, and I need to talk to you about some people I think should be interviewed for your staff."

Several months earlier, at one of the BGEA board meetings, Graham indicated that he wanted to have a more integrated staff. Since that meeting, Hill, who had extensive contacts within the black evangelical community, had been busy identifying qualified candidates.

Hill and Graham first met during the 1963 Los Angeles Crusade. During the next few years, Hill followed the course of Billy's activities and the growth of his ministry. Although the two men weren't in touch personally, Hill was very interested in Graham's position on the race issue. Having heard conflicting appraisals of Graham, Hill wanted to find out for himself where the evangelist stood on this crucial national question. Then, in 1969, Graham was in Anaheim, California, for a crusade. Hill, who was an important local pastor, was invited by the crusade committee to offer a prayer during one of the services. After the benediction, Hill, who was seated behind Graham, tapped him on the shoulder and blurted out, "Billy, I've got to talk to you!" And to his great surprise, Graham replied, "I've got to talk to you!"

A week later, Hill was summoned to Huntington Beach, where Graham was resting following the crusade. He drove to the resort determined "to actually know Billy Graham. I had heard much about him from others, but I never look at a person through other people's eyeglasses; I use my own." Although the appointment was scheduled to last thirty minutes, the two men sat together for over four hours. "We prayed together, we cried together, we became friends; and I've been a close-up supporter ever since," Hill said.

Now, sitting on the couch in Graham's suite, Hill told the evangelist how delighted he was to see so many blacks at the service the previous evening. He also said:

I've been spending my time meeting with the brothers. A lot of my brothers have many questions about you, Billy. They want to know about your true intentions and whether the Graham organization is trying to engulf us as a race. I say to them, "You have to understand Billy Graham as being involved in a four-base ministry. The first-base ministry is reconciling man to God, but once you've reached first, you don't turn right and go back into the dugout. You turn left and go onto second base, where reconciled men under God become reconciled one to another. But you can't stay on second and make love all day, because at third base we hear the cries of the poor and hungry, and if we did not move on to third, we would make a farce of our reconciliation. So we move to third and try to ameliorate human distress, but we don't stop there because Billy has a home-plate ministry and that's to anticipate the coming of the Lord, to know that we are heavenbound—that's home plate."

"You remember, Billy, I predicted this would probably be your most integrated crusade. The reason I said this is that the true story of the South has not been told," Hill added, noting that, "The last time I was in Jackson, Mississippi, was with the Freedom Riders. It's a long way from this hotel to where I stayed in those days."

Billy laughed. Then, turning serious, he said, "Ed, you have been a tremendous blessing to our work, and I know you have met with a number of pastors to explain my ministry and my reasons for coming to Jackson. I so much appreciate all you have done." They then turned to the names on Hill's list.

QUESTION OF INTEGRATION

I excused myself and wandered down to the lobby, where I hoped to meet Dr. Hill after his appointment with Billy. I, too, remembered what Jackson used to be like. It was widely recognized as the last major stronghold of resistance to the growing current of racial change that was alive throughout the nation. I was interested in speaking with Dr. Hill and learning of his impressions of the crusade and its impact on integration in Jackson.

Twenty-five minutes later, when Hill emerged from the elevator, I approached him. He remembered seeing me in Billy's suite, and I introduced myself. When I asked if he had a few minutes to talk, he nodded and we went up to his room. I knew instinctively that I could be totally frank with Hill—there was no guile or pretense about the man. He also had a no-nonsense aura about him, so I quickly came to the point. Although the crusade was impressively integrated, I asked if he thought the euphoria of these eight days would last through the months and years ahead.

Mississippi had played a major role in the history of racial violence in the United States during the 1950s and '60s. It saw the lynching of fourteen-year-old Emmett Till, the murder of three civil rights workers in Philadelphia, the furor caused by the matriculation of James Meredith at the University of Mississippi, and the murder of civil rights leader Medgar Evers. In 1970, it also saw the tragic slaying of two black students at Jackson State during an anti-war protest.

Given this background of violence, I asked Hill if he thought it was possible for Billy Graham to make an impact on the course of race relations in the state. Looking me in the eye, Hill said:

> The answer to your question is yes. I don't know of any other movement which does as much lasting good in a community as a Billy Graham Crusade. I don't know of anything else that touches as many people as a Graham Crusade. A year ago, people who didn't know each other started praying together, started studying together, and started planning together; it brought people together along racial lines. Now you see integration in the choir, on the platform, in stands. We've talked about it in the past—we said it ought to happen, it needs to happen—but somehow the Billy Graham Evangelical Association has made it happen.

Hill's words echoed those of local black and white clergy-men. Black minister Herman Pride, the crusade treasurer, commented on the value of prayer groups, saying, "This has been the first time that many black people have entered white churches. They have begun to know one another. The Crusade has brought them together." Another crusade official, Dr. S.L. Bowman, long active in civil rights, stated, "People have gotten to know each other across racial lines. This had not happened prior to the Crusade." When asked to comment on the Jackson Crusade's racial aspects, the Reverend Donald Patterson, pastor of the all-white First Presbyterian Church, said, "We have blacks and whites on our committee, and we have been blessed by God with a good relationship. The Crusade has helped us move in the right direction."

"But," I insisted to Hill, "what of the future? Will these pastors continue to meet together? Or will they go their own way, as it has been in the past?" Hill responded forcefully, saying:

When we leave here, normal problems will crop up, but we now have a precedent and when problems occur, the people here can say, "We worked together on the Billy Graham Crusade; we can work together on this." I think the Crusade has established an open door for black and white pastors to relate.

I turned the focus of the conversation on Graham himself. I was curious to hear what Hill thought of Graham, the man. Hill didn't know the evangelist back in the "old days," when most of the relationships and allegiances involved with Graham and his team members had been formed. He was in a position to be more objective in his evaluation:

I've been around a lot of people in and out of the church who have experienced considerable success, and I've learned that there is something about success and power which tends to corrupt. But when you look at the Billy Graham Association, when you look at Billy, when you look at Ruth and their children, when you go into their homes, when you knock on the door, you expect to meet someone who supercedes the Apostle Paul, a holier-than-thou, and here comes a smiling, down-home person from North Carolina who just grabs you and says "Hello, brother." You're shocked, but it's a glad shock. On the one hand, you expected someone you would bow to; on the other hand you have someone you can say to, "Hey, give me a piece of chicken." And I think this is why God has chosen to continue to use him. I believe it is those who remain simple and down to earth and humble and touchable that He has chosen to manifest His glory through.

And I'll tell you something else. Billy has the lowest ratings of Billy Graham of any polls that have been taken. I don't know anyone who is more critical of Billy Graham than Billy Graham himself. When I first realized this, I thought he was jiving me, but this was not so; this man does not do things with the certainty that: I'm Billy Graham and people are going to listen to me. I don't think he's ever had the thought: Well, I'm Billy Graham and I'm going to Rio, and 200,000 people are going to meet me there and I'm going to slay them. His attitude is: Well, we will do good if 20,000 show up.

I asked Hill what he believed enabled Graham to be a pacesetter, to move his constituents forward on key theological and social issues. Smiling, he leaned forward in his chair and said:

Look, I think Billy is often surprised himself at what he says and does. There are often aftershocks that follow his actions, but the true man of God, when questioned as to whether he really meant to say or do a certain thing, says, "Yes, I did mean it," while the fake says, "Well, wait a minute—that action needs interpretation." Billy, as a true servant of God, listens for His voice and has the courage to say and do what God has told him.

Finally, I asked Dr. Hill how long he believed Billy could or would maintain his ministry; how long he would continue to preach and hold crusades. Hill responded:

Time and circumstances are going to keep Billy involved in crusades, whether he wants to or not. The nation has lost confidence in many institutions, but Billy has retained his credibility. And people, especially young people, will continue to talk to Billy, and Billy's going to constantly respond to them. I don't think he wants this responsibility. I can't really blame him because it's an awesome responsibility, but being the kind of man he is, and knowing the way he walks with God, he will continue to speak out, and he will keep busy for a long time to come.

I was very impressed with Dr. Hill, and understood why Graham allied himself with him. Their relationship was one more example of Graham's inclination to bring highly competent people into his organization. Other black colleagues have also made important contributions to Graham's ministry, including Ralph Bell, Howard Jones, and Norman Sanders. They and other blacks who were close to the Graham organization intuitively trusted Billy and were very much aware of his behind-the-scenes efforts on behalf of the black struggle for racial equality.

In the late 1960s, for example, Graham had invited about twenty black church leaders to meet with him in New York for a frank, off-the-record discussion of their problems. During that session, several of those in attendance expressed their concern over the Nixon administration's plan to cut off funds for social welfare projects. They were further frustrated because they were not able to communicate directly with the president. Responding to their concerns, Graham arranged for a number of those church leaders to meet with President Nixon in the White House. The meeting resulted in the reinstatement of significant funding for programs in black neighborhoods.

One participant in the Oval Office meeting that day was Reverend John Williams from Kansas City. Williams, who eventually became a member of the BGEA board, told the president that the funds needed to complete a hospital in his area had been frozen. Two days later, Williams received word that the Department of Health, Education and Welfare had approved a $1 million grant for the project. And today, the Martin Luther King Hospital provides vital services to the black community of Kansas City.

On the other hand, Graham's stand on the racial issue cost him both friends and contributions. When Howard Jones first came on staff, Graham received a number of letters asking why he was associating with "niggers." In response to these slurs, Graham made a special point of introducing Jones at meetings and receptions. Jones recalled the words spoken to Billy by the late Martin Luther King, Jr.: "I believe your crusades are doing more to break down racial barriers and to bring the races together than what I'm doing. Your work is helping me."

It should be remembered that American churches were segregated well into the 1960s; it was said that 11 AM Sunday was the most segregated hour of the week. And evangelical churches were especially prone to discrimination—due in part to the generally accepted notion that the Bible taught that blacks were inherently inferior to whites.

Billy Graham, who had grown up in a region that was highly permeated by such teachings, wouldn't learn of the fallacy of that notion until he attended Wheaton College. There, he learned from anthropology professor Dr. George Horner that there was no scientific basis for the theory of black inferiority. It was a lesson that Billy would never forget, and when he conducted a four-week crusade in Jackson in 1952, he insisted on integrated seating. He also made a number of comments on race during that crusade that caused consternation within both the city and state power structures. In fact, the then-governor, Hugh White, was so upset that he telephoned Graham, urging him to stop speaking out on the issue.

Billy Graham did not, of course, heed the governor's advice.

7

Midday Agenda

By THE TIME I LEFT DR. HILL AND GOT back to the suite, it was about 2:30. Billy was in the middle of a meeting with Sterling Huston, the team member responsible for scheduling all of Graham's crusades and speaking engagements in North America. A thirty-five-year-old native of Maine, Huston, like many of his colleagues, came to the BGEA from the professional ranks of Youth for Christ. He was an engineer with a master of science degree, and had several years of business experience with major corporations. Huston handled the majority of the more than 8,000 annual requests for Graham's public appearances, and was responsible for the exploration, preparation, function, and follow-up regarding both crusades and speaking engagements. In most of the cases, he was also the person who had to deny these requests.

Recently, Huston found himself declining more invitations than usual because of Graham's need to limit his schedule. Billy simply could not go for sixteen weeks at a stretch, as he did in the first New York City Crusade, nor was he able to preach two or three times a day, as he was once used to doing. Still, Graham usually conducted five major crusades a year, two or three in the United States, and the others in such major international centers as West Germany, Hong Kong, and Australia. He spoke at college and university commencements, as well as important religious gatherings, including the annual meeting of the Southern Baptist Convention. He also delivered sermons from key pulpits, such as the one in New York City's Riverside Church.

He presided over the quarterly meetings of the Billy Graham Evangelistic Association, and spent many days each year attending board meetings of institutions such as Gordon College and Divinity School, and visiting projects that were administered by members of his team. Before 1975 was over, Billy would also speak to more than a thousand atomic scientists at Los Alamos—the first time this influential group was addressed by a clergyman.

Part of each week was also given over to Graham's *Hour of Decision* radio broadcast. And in any given week, several hours were devoted to the writing of his newspaper column. Billy also spent time writing occasional magazine articles and books. In addition, there were visits with family and friends; meetings with political, social, and economic leaders; and many hours of study and meditation—both for personal spiritual needs and in preparation for the many sermons and messages he delivered throughout the year.

Sterling Huston wrote regular brief memos to Billy, keeping him abreast of the latest information on scheduling, as well as on the progress of planning for coming engagements. It was in response to one of these memoranda that Huston was called to the suite that day. Billy wanted more information concerning his appearance in August at the National Convention of the American Bar Association. He had been invited on two earlier occasions, but had not been able to accept either time. Huston told Billy that the ABA date was firm. He then advised Billy of the progress of the Washington, DC Crusade, which was scheduled for mid-1976.

BICENTENNIAL OBSERVANCE AND SPIRITUAL RENEWAL

Graham was especially interested in the nation's bicentennial observance. He planned to spend all of 1976 in the United States, and had been swamped with requests to participate in related events. He hoped the observance would result in the return to those religious principles that he believed were basic to the founding and development of the nation.

This was a sensitive area for Graham, who had often been accused of promoting what the sociologist Robert Bellah called "American Civil Religion." Billy's participation in White House religious services during the Nixon years, as well as his leadership in the evangelical campaign known as "Key '73," led some critics to charge that he promoted a religion of "Americanism." Graham refuted these assertions, saying that his ministry was of worldwide dimension and that he did not represent the United States or any other nation. Rather, he referred to himself as an "Ambassador for Christ."

There was a fine line here between Graham's patriotism and love of country and the somewhat jingoistic events with which he was sometimes associated. A case in point was his cosponsorship in 1970, along with comedian Bob Hope and Reader's Digest President Hobart Lewis, of "Honor America Day." This Washington-based celebration, replete with a morning religious service and an evening fireworks display, was aimed at expressing what was right with America at a time when many people—the youth in particular—were discovering things that were wrong.

Carrying his message to the thousands of people assembled at the Lincoln Memorial, Graham called his audience and the nation to spiritual renewal. Others, however, including then-President Nixon, used Honor America Day to "prove" that all was well with America's society. Graham indicated to me that his bicentennial activities would not be open to the charge that he equated Christianity with American values.

TEAM ATTITUDE

Huston and Billy also discussed some personnel matters. Characteristically, members of the Graham organization possessed both professional expertise and deep spiritual commitment. When I asked Huston what he looked for in a prospective member, he replied that the Graham ministry had a sense of mission; therefore, the person considered for the position "must be motivated by his commitment to Christ." The candidate also had to have an attitude that was "consistent with the spirit and drive that Mr. Graham exemplified."

I asked if such criteria would encourage potential team members to attempt to imitate Graham. Responding quickly, Huston said that that was the last thing Billy would want. "We're not looking for 'little Billy Grahams,'" he explained, "but, rather, for men who have a sense of woe if they do not preach the Gospel." I found Huston's response interesting. Over the years, while I had come across many preachers and church workers who—whether consciously or not—affected many of Graham's mannerisms and vocal inflections, I could not think of a single team member whose public or private life was modeled on Billy's.

Huston also said that the Graham organization looked for people who made a good appearance—"not that appearance makes one a better man, but it reduces the limitations a man faces if he is to present himself well." Team members and the immediate support staff were neatly groomed, tastefully dressed, and had cheerful demeanors.

Q. What is your favorite extended Bible passage?

A. *The Fifteenth Chapter of Luke, which is the story of the "Prodigal Son."*

I mentioned that the people around Billy Graham seemed serene and appeared to derive much satisfaction from their work. Huston explained that the team members found the qualities of honesty, sincerity, and dedication in Billy, and believed that being with him was exactly where God wanted them to be. They were involved in an exciting and productive ministry—one in which God had called on Billy to accomplish great things.

During my many conversations with Graham, I was struck by the number of times he praised members of his staff. I was also impressed by the team members' loyalty to Billy. While his associates did not hesitate to acknowledge his weak points or constructively criticize his performance, they were also his most loyal supporters. Their continued relationship with Billy, despite attractive offers to go elsewhere, was perhaps the greatest testament to his leadership and ability to maintain the proper tone for the work of his organization.

Huston summed up the team's attitude by observing, "When you're related to someone whom God has particularly chosen, and he has been generous and gracious, there's not a lot of room for conflict."

"RUNNING THE RACE"

When Huston left, I asked Billy if he was frustrated over having to refuse so many invitations and speaking opportunities. He responded by saying that he did feel enormous pressure and was unhappy that he could not visit so many of the areas of the world that urgently requested his presence. He realized, however, that Jesus's active ministry lasted only three years; yet, when He went to the cross, He was able to say, "It is finished."

I got the impression that despite the frustrations, Graham believed that he was "running the race," described by Paul in the New Testament, to the best of his intellectual ability and physical capacity. He also felt certain that whatever he did was directed by God as the result of prayer and the leading of the Holy Spirit. Therefore, he would never say, "We should have gone to Dallas last month instead of Munich." He might, however, linger over a decision regarding an appearance, gathering input and advice before making a commitment. But once the decision has been made, he holds to it and gives the assignment his very best effort.

Some people—even those who stood a good chance of extending Billy an invitation that he might accept—are often inhibited in their petitions. Assuming that he could not possibly accept due to his fame and harried schedule, they don't even extend their invitations. Such assumptions can sometimes lead to misunderstandings, as I learned firsthand.

Billy and I knew had a mutual acquaintance, a religious leader. This person invited a member of the Graham Team, rather than Billy himself, to address a theological colloquium. When Billy found out, he asked me if the official was angry with him. And if so, why? I assured Billy that the religious leader was not upset with him. Rather, he didn't want to put Billy on the spot by inviting him to attend a function that wasn't likely to have a high priority. Billy understood. It caused me to wonder, however, if Billy really comprehended the wariness that developed in those who had knowledge of his complex ministry, with its great demands on his time.

Having said that, it sometimes took a good measure of old-fashioned *chutzpa* to ask Billy for an appointment. And yet, in most cases, a person knew intuitively that he would respond positively, regardless of the pressures involved. I had that experience several years ago while working for the American Jewish Committee. I met Rivka Alexandrovich, a Soviet Jewish woman from the city of Riga, who came to the United States. Her goal was to win public support for her daughter, Ruth, who was a prisoner of conscience in Russia.

I called Billy and reached him in the barbershop of the Madison Hotel in Washington, DC. After hearing of Mrs. Alexandrovich's need, Billy wanted to meet her. He asked me to bring her to Chicago, where he would be the following week. The meeting was very emotional. The positive energy in the room was undeniable as Billy carefully jotted down pertinent details, while expressing great sympathy for young Ruth Alexandrovich's plight.

He then strode over to the telephone, paged through his address book, and dialed. "Is Henry there?" he asked. "Well, please tell him to call me the minute he comes in." No one in that room had to ask who "Henry" was; the call had been made to a number in Key Biscayne, Florida, where Secretary of State Henry Kissinger was meeting with President Nixon. Five minutes later, the telephone rang. It was Kissinger. Graham briefed him on the situation, and then asked if there was something he could do for Ruth Alexandrovich.

Later that evening, Billy issued a statement calling attention to the plight of Soviet Jewry. Two months later, Ruth Alexandrovich would leave Russia and land at Lod Airport, near Tel Aviv, Israel.

HIGH DEMANDS OF A TELECAST

I looked at my watch and discovered it was 3:11. I excused myself, telling Billy that I would see him later before leaving for the stadium. It was hardly a magnanimous gesture on my part; I had been told in advance that Billy needed two hours in the afternoon to rest and prepare for his evening message. He used the time to unwind from the activities of the day and look over his notes, making any necessary changes to the sermon. It was especially important to do so on that day, as his evening message was going to be taped for television.

When Billy prepared for the televising of a sermon, he memorized his message, so that he could look directly into the camera's lens. He also had to be extremely careful in what he said, as his message would eventually be viewed in many parts of the world by audiences that differed nationally, ethnically, and racially. He had to be sure to drop all local references, as people viewing the broadcast in India or Latin America could not be expected to know where Jackson was located, let alone understand Billy's meaning when he spoke of "Ole Miss." Billy also had to articulate a message that would be theologically clear to people of varied spiritual backgrounds.

Given the demands of the medium, and because the broadcast ministry represented an enormous investment of time, effort, and money, Billy and his associates were under great strain on the crusade days that were televised. Even Billy's closest associates couldn't fully comprehend the physical, mental, and emotional toll it took to preach before a camera. Once, during a crusade in Norfolk, Virginia, Billy became ill and was unable to get to the auditorium for one of the services. Grady Wilson, who substituted for Billy, vividly recalled how taxing it was to speak to an audience that was not only local and live, but also being taped for worldwide television viewers.

"UNDILUTED ENTHUSIASM"

After leaving Billy, I planned to head back to my room at the Jackson Hilton, which was also the location of the team headquarters. When I returned to the lobby, I ran into Harold Lindsell, who was also heading to the Hilton, so we shared a taxi.

Earlier, Lindsell had had a fifteen-minute meeting with Graham, and while their conversation was privileged, Lindsell told me that the evangelist was very troubled over the world situation. Not only was he worried about the future of America's involvement in the Pacific and on the Asian continent, he was concerned over renewed hostilities in the Middle East.

As we drove through the streets of Jackson, I couldn't help thinking about Graham, who was in his suite, getting ready for the evening's meeting. After all the places he's been, all the experiences he's had, all the great and near-great people he's met, wasn't it something of a letdown to come to a city like Jackson? Didn't he have to psych himself up to conduct a crusade here? When I expressed these feelings to Lindsell, he agreed that Jackson was surely not one of the garden spots of the world. And its challenges and opportunities were different from those Graham would encounter in, say, Japan or South Africa or Germany. However, Lindsell described Billy as having "undiluted enthusiasm—a man who genuinely relishes getting up in the morning, who lives with a constant air of expectancy." Thus, every crusade or appearance had meaning and purpose.

From a practical point of view, it was also very important for Graham to appear from time to time in the Bible Belt. Jackson was very fertile territory with a tremendous density of evangelical Christians within a 200-mile radius. It was vital for Graham to touch base from time to time with the core element of his constituency.

TEAM HEADQUARTERS

Our cab pulled up to the Hilton, and we found the lobby to be noisy and crowded. I soon discovered the reason for the commotion—Johnny Cash, June Carter, and their entourage had just arrived. They were quickly hustled into an elevator and the din died down.

The Cashes and the Grahams were close personal friends, and Johnny performed at Graham crusades whenever his crowded schedule permitted. Cash's appearance in Jackson was not a simple matter of his flying into town with a few backup musicians. He took crusades very seriously. That evening, he would have twenty people with him on the platform. He also brought all of the sound and lighting equipment he normally used at a major, paid performance. In fact, a huge truck was unloaded at the stadium and a crew of technicians set up the complicated equipment used for Cash's performance.

In the lobby, I recognized Don Bailey, Billy's press representative. I had met Don a month earlier while spending the day with Billy at his home in Montreat. He walked over to us with a young woman and introduced her as Claire Beversluis, the legislative secretary to Arizona's Senator Barry Goldwater. Claire and her family had rededicated their lives to Christ in 1969 during the Madison Square Garden Crusade. Since then, she had become an ardent supporter of Graham, and spent her vacations attending meetings and helping out with office and counseling chores. The Jackson Crusade was her sixth.

There were many others who regularly attended Graham crusades. Neither hero worshippers nor camp followers, they simply enjoyed the fellowship and spiritual nourishment of a crusade. One old-timer, Peck Gunn, the self-styled poet laureate of Tennessee, brought along a busload of friends to every U.S. crusade, and his Tennessee ham breakfast was a must for the team.

If the Graham Team was a "family," Claire Beversluis, Peck Gunn, and the other regular crusade attendees were the "extended Graham family." They brought a spirit of camaraderie, as well as a welcome reservoir of familiar faces to crusades throughout the country.

By 4:30, the traffic within the hotel lobby started to grow as team members began returning from their afternoon engagements.

Howard Jones had been at the Parchman State Penitentiary, where he preached to 800 convicts, of which 200 had committed to Christ; Lee Fisher walked through the lobby carrying the accordion with which he had just entertained patients at a local nursing home; Walter Smyth spent the afternoon meeting with Baptist officials, briefing them on the international aspects of the Graham ministry; and Cliff Barrows and Grady Wilson had conducted a series of meetings with those who could not be accommodated in Graham's schedule.

FINAL PREPARATIONS FOR THE SERVICE

Meanwhile, in the pressroom on the hotel's second floor, Arthur Matthews spoke on the telephone with a UPI reporter in Washington, while Don Bailey sifted through interview requests from several national magazines. Two doors away, T.W. Wilson and Charlie Riggs went over the evening's program. T.W. was concerned about the weather—the sun had receded and ominous-looking dark clouds were building in the western sky. For the past three weeks, Jackson had been inundated with rain. For a time, it appeared that the stadium infield would be too muddy for those who wanted to come forward during the service. Then two days before the beginning of the crusade, the skies cleared and the warm sun appeared.

It seemed, however, that the skies were about to open up again, which would have a strong impact on attendance. If the rain began in the next hour or so, many of those who had planned on coming would likely stay home. If the rain held off until the evening service was underway, the crowd might be uncomfortable, but at least it would be there in the stadium. Whether it rained or not, there would still be a base attendance of about 20,000 folks who had made advance reservations and would be arriving by bus.

The weather notwithstanding, a genuine sense of excitement and drama was building in the greater Jackson area. Thousands of men, women, and children were returning home from work and school in eager anticipation of attending the evening's service. In thousands of other homes, crusade volunteers—ushers, counselors, choir members, and Co-Labor corps members—were eating early suppers and making last-minute preparations for the drive to the stadium.

In the coffee shop of the Jackson Hilton, several team members were enjoying a light snack, while over at the Holiday Inn, the man who had begun his day with prayer was back on his knees, asking God to grant him a full measure of liberty and power for the message he was about to deliver. When he had finished his prayers, Billy turned on the television to watch the five o'clock news. He was distressed to learn that a group of pirates had seized the *Mayaguez,* an American merchant vessel sailing in Cambodian waters.

Billy then called my room at the Hilton, reminding me to meet Grady at 5:50 in front of the Holiday Inn for a ride to the stadium. He then added, almost as an afterthought, "Things are a lot more hectic today, Jerry, than when you were at the house." I was so stunned by his thoughtfulness in calling that I was able only to mumble, "Yes, it has been busy." Our conversation ended. I walked over to the window, and as I watched the clouds gathering on the near horizon, I anxiously awaited the evening that lay ahead.

Crusade executive committee chairman and former Bengal's football star Anthony Muñoz sits beside Billy at the 2002 Cincinnati Mission. Billy's son Franklin looks on from behind.

8

Toward the Arena

At 5:45, I FOUND GRADY STANDING beside his Pontiac in the driveway of the Holiday Inn. "I just called upstairs," he said. "Billy will be down in a few minutes." As we stood and talked, a dark-colored automobile with four plainclothes detectives pulled up behind us. They would be escorting us to the stadium.

As the crusade was in its fourth day, I asked Grady his impressions of how it was going so far. He was clearly pleased. He felt the crowds had been large and enthusiastic. He also reminisced:

> What you see here is a far cry from the old days. I remember our very first crusade. It was held in Charlotte at the National Guard Armory. The meetings lasted for three weeks. And the last night, Gil Dodds, the Olympic track star, ran around the indoor track, then changed clothes, and gave his testimony. This attracted 2,000 persons and we thought we were really big stuff. Then we went to Miami and started in a church, had to move to a larger sanctuary, and finally, we ended up at the Bayfront auditorium. From there it was the Lyric Theater in Baltimore, where a crowd of 2,800 came out the last night. Today, we sometimes have twice that number come forward, or sing in the choir.

I asked Grady if he had ever thought back in those early days that the ministry would develop and, indeed, mushroom as it had. "No, we could never have imagined life would turn out this way," he replied. "You see, Billy and T.W. and I used to throw rocks at each other when we were boys. Billy was a very regular normal guy. In fact, he was actually about the most shy and timid guy in Charlotte. Now I see him preach before thousands of people, or hear him praised by a president or a king, and no one could ever have predicted it would be like this. Why, even his girlfriend at Bible school in Florida dropped him because she wanted to marry someone who would be a successful minister."

When I asked Grady how he accounted for Graham's incredible success, he responded by saying, "The answer is the sovereignty of God asserting itself in this generation." He continued, "We live in an age when frustration, uncertainty, and the multitude of problems we face on a human level are driving people to seek spiritual answers. Billy Graham has been consistent as to the remedy for these problems."

As Grady spoke, Billy and T.W. approached the car and Billy joked, "Jerry, you had better be careful with what Grady tells you." We all laughed and got into the car. I marveled at the easy rapport among the three old friends. They had been through so many experiences together—both rewarding and difficult. They moved beyond the constricted circles of Charlotte and the old-time South of their boyhoods, yet they never allowed fame and good fortune to diminish their mutual esteem and respect.

I felt a sense of satisfaction in thinking that these three men, all approaching the end of middle age, still appreciated one another and thought it was the most natural thing in the world to be together. Their relationship, as well as Billy's longstanding connection with people like Cliff Barrows and George Beverly Shea, offered insight into one of the major reasons for the stability of the Graham organization. Many of its key people were there from the beginning, when no one expected Billy Graham to emerge as a world-famous religious leader.

TRAILER HEADQUARTERS

During the ride to the stadium, Billy was preoccupied with the *Mayaguez* incident. Recalling his late afternoon conversation with

Harold Lindsell, he asked T.W. to get the latest information on the seizure.

In an effort to take Billy's mind off the *Mayaguez*, Grady described a meeting he had had earlier with the mother of the pastor of Albuquerque's First Baptist Church. She told Grady that her son, who had been active in the recent crusade in that city, had been converted to Christ during the first Jackson Crusade back in 1953. "Yes," Billy said, "He's doing a fine job in Albuquerque, and I'm delighted he came to Christ under my ministry." Then T.W. reminded Billy that Johnny Cash would be visiting him in his trailer around 6:45. He also mentioned several others who would be seeing Billy prior to the service.

Billy usually arrived at the crusade site about an hour before the service was scheduled to begin, and used a trailer as his field headquarters. There, he greeted guests, took important phone calls, and made last-minute preparations for the evening's meeting. From a security standpoint, having a trailer on site allowed him to enter the meeting area long before the arrival of most of his audience.

About ten minutes after our departure from the hotel, Grady turned onto Woodrow Wilson Avenue, and made a right turn past the stadium's main parking lot. He drove to the end zone on the east side of the field, and pulled up next to the white and silver trailer that was parked just behind the stands. Billy walked quickly into the trailer, while Grady and T.W. joined Sterling Huston and Don Bailey, who were waiting near the entrance of a tunnel that led under the stands to the platform that served as a stage. All four wore bronze lapel buttons that gave them access to the platform, and carried walkie-talkies, so they could communicate with one another throughout the evening.

I took a quick tour of the infield. A small army of technicians was setting up the television lights and checking out camera locations. Others were testing the sound system, while at the press table, two of Cash's people were installing a control panel for the singer's special audio setup. And on the platform itself, workmen were erecting a canopy to protect the area from the possible rain.

This evening was the crusade's Youth Night. In recent years, there had been one or two such events during each crusade. Billy was very concerned about reaching young people with his message. He had always been quite successful in holding their attention and winning their allegiance—a rapport that T.W. claimed was built on "genuine frankness and compassion." T.W. further observed, "These youngsters are seeking idols, whether they be sports stars, astronauts, or rock musicians. Billy is able to present the person of Christ as an attractive and viable alternative to the usual run of teenage heroes."

ETHEL WATERS, JOHNNY CASH, AND JUNE CARTER

I walked over to the trailer and found Billy, who was immaculately dressed in a dark blue suit, white shirt, and blue tie, talking with Ethel Waters. The venerable singer had been a close friend of Billy's ever since the first New York Crusade in 1957.

Miss Waters sang her famous "His Eye is on the Sparrow" during the service held the evening before. Although her vocal power may have dimmed over the years, she retained her innate showmanship and received a standing ovation at the end of the song. She then addressed the crowd:

> In 1957, I, Ethel Waters, a 380-pound decrepit old lady, rededicated my life to Jesus Christ, and boy, because He lives, just look at me now. I tell you because He lives; and because my precious child, Billy, gave me the opportunity to stand there, I can thank God for the chance to tell you His eye is on all of us sparrows.

That night in the trailer, Ethel looked radiant as she spoke with Billy; she exuded a tremendous sense of personal dignity. The two friends discussed the progress of the Jackson Crusade, and Billy asked Miss Waters to join him in September at Lubbock. "You know if I can, I'll be there. I so much enjoy being at a crusade," she said. "Now I have to go up and join the choir rehearsal or Cliff will be wondering where I am." Billy rose from the couch and helped Miss Waters to the door, where two young women waited to escort her to the choir section.

A minute or so later, the door opened and Ken Chafin walked in with a middle-aged gentleman. Ken said, "Dr. Graham, I would like you to meet Reverend Harold Johnson, who is attending the School of Evangelism. You may remember that he wrote a note to you earlier in the week." Extending his hand in greeting, Billy said, "Yes, of course. Please sit down." Johnson expressed how much being at the crusade and the School of Evangelism meant to him. After a few minutes of conversation, Billy asked him to lead them in a word of prayer, during which Johnson asked for "a harvest of souls this evening." When he finished, I noticed a tear forming in the corner of his eye. "God bless you, brother," Billy said to Johnson as he left the trailer.

I learned later that the Reverend Johnson had written to Graham, describing his frustration with the ministry. He also said that he was about to leave his church and, quite likely, take a secular position. The evening before, he had come to the service with a delegation from the School of Evangelism, and when the invitation was extended, he came forward to rededicate his life to Christ.

Billy went to the refrigerator and took out a carafe of ice water. His walkie-talkie crackled. It was Sterling Huston informing him that the Cashes had just reached the stadium and were coming directly to the trailer. Billy was very pleased. Johnny "is a wonderful man. Ruth and I have been in the Cash home," he told me, "and we have felt the Christian atmosphere and the warmth Johnny and June provide for their children. It's also been our joy to have them visit us in Montreat."

When the Cashes arrived, the two men embraced and June kissed Billy on the cheek. Billy wanted to know if they were being taken care of properly—were their rooms comfortable? Had the arrangements for their performances been adequate? Cash assured Billy that everything was fine, and said how happy he and June were to be in Jackson. "I'm only sorry we have to leave so soon," he said, "but this recording session has been planned for weeks now." Billy understood; he knew how complicated a person's schedule could become. He was genuinely grateful that they were able to come at all.

I was intrigued by the scene in the trailer. Here were people who were famous products of the South. When they were growing up, no one could have imagined that they would one day appear together before thousands to bear witness to and preach their faith. It was also true that their backgrounds were quite different—Billy's was middle class while Cash came from a poor family—but in their hearts they were quite similar. Despite all the miles they have traveled and the towns they have visited and conquered, they were very much at home in Jackson. They knew that the people who were now gathering in the Memorial Stadium understood them and took pride in their success.

Soon it was time for June and Johnny to join their accompanists. Billy walked them to the door, and as they made their way toward the stadium, Billy waved and said, "I'll see you on the platform."

EMERGENCY RELIEF FUND

T.W. came into the trailer and informed Billy that he had been in touch with the local office of the National Weather Service. He reported the disheartening forecast—"Radar shows heavy showers falling fifteen miles southwest of Jackson, and there should be a downpour in the stadium area in about one hour." Billy asked T.W. to make sure his raincoat was handy, then he picked up the telephone and dialed the team office, which was located under the stands. He was looking for Howard Jones, and wanted to meet with him. Within a few minutes, Jones was inside the trailer.

First, Billy asked how the meeting at the State Penitentiary went earlier that day and was pleased with Jones's report. Reverend Howard Jones, an outstanding preacher, conducted several major crusades in Africa. In addition to his evangelistic responsibilities, Jones had been designated by Billy to direct the BGEA's recently instituted Emergency Relief Fund, which, Jones recalled, came into being during the Twin Cities Crusade in 1973. Billy had approached him before one of the meetings and said, "Howard, I'm going to raise some real money tonight to feed the hungry in Africa." When he spoke, Billy announced his intention to start the program, and the offering that evening totaled $71,000. Since that experience in Minneapolis, Graham has made other appeals for the Emergency Relief Fund during crusades, but only after the funds for the crusade budget have been raised.

Unlike the humanitarian gestures made by other evangelical organizations, there are no strings attached to grants from the Emergency Relief Fund. The money is channeled through existing, reputable agencies—no hungry person has to listen to a sermon before receiving assistance. The rationale behind the program can be understood by reading the words printed on each Emergency Fund check that is issued by the Association: "Given in the name of the Lord Jesus Christ."

When one considers the long-standing evangelical reluctance to engage in social action projects, the establishment of the Emergency Relief Fund is nothing short of courageous, bringing to mind the "third base" ministry articulated by Dr. E.V. Hill. And it is graphic proof of Graham's capacity to move beyond the narrow structures of twentieth-century American evangelicalism.

The failure of Graham's predecessors and peers in the American evangelical movement to become involved with social reform is aberrant. Nineteenth-century English evangelical leaders, such as John Newton and William Wilberforce, had worked toward the abolition of the slave trade, as well as industrial and prison reform. A committed Scottish evangelist had founded the British Labour Party. In the United States during the 1800s, revivalist

Q. Do you have a favorite spectator sport?

A. *I go to a ball game once in a while; I love that. I love basketball; I love baseball. I try to keep up with the various teams in football.*

George Whitefield collected funds for orphans, free blacks, and immigrants during his open-air meetings. Ohio's Oberlin College, under the leadership of Charles Finney, the great mid-nineteenth-century evangelist, became a center of abolitionist activity.

In developing a program of humanitarian concern, Graham has influenced a new generation of leadership, including his son Franklin.

FINAL MOMENTS BEFORE THE SERVICE

Billy and Reverend Jones finished their conversation, and Jones left to join his three daughters, who performed as a vocal trio at many of the crusades. Billy radioed Don Bailey and asked if there was any further information on the *Mayaguez* incident. I mentioned my earlier conversation with Howard Lindsell regarding world turmoil, and Billy reiterated his belief that events were moving toward a flashpoint:

> I really believe the coming of Christ may be much nearer than we think. I have a deep sense of urgency about my preaching; I want to reach so many people at this time of crisis.

Billy then mentioned several areas of the world that were on the verge of exploding into open conflict. He was particularly concerned with conditions in the Middle East, where he had recently visited and met with officials in both Egypt and Israel. I had joined Billy during the day-and-a-half he had spent in the Jewish State, and we reminisced about several aspects of that experience . . .

9

Flashback to the Holy Land

Olympic flight 130 from Athens was five minutes early as it landed flawlessly at David Ben Gurion Airport outside Tel Aviv. Billy Graham and his associates Grady Wilson and Walter Smyth stepped from the aircraft, and were met by their colleague Roy Gustafson, who had led Christian visitors on hundreds of tours to Israel. Also waiting on the tarmac to meet the evangelist was David Ben Dov, the then-director of the North American section of the Israeli Foreign Ministry.

Although Billy looked tanned and fit, he was still feeling the aftereffects of a serious case of food poisoning, which he had suffered a few days earlier in Cairo. In fact, the sudden illness had almost caused Graham to cancel his visit to Israel. However, his determination to make the journey, combined with a strict diet and loads of antibiotics, enabled the evangelist to arrive in the Jewish State on schedule.

Billy and his group were ushered into a sleek black Mercedes limousine, which would be transporting them through their whirlwind tour of Israel during the next day and a half. Their first stop was in the airport's VIP lounge, where they waited for their passports and other documents to be cleared. There, Billy was also interviewed by a reporter for Israel radio. The evangelist indicated that this visit—his first trip to Israel in several years—was in response to an invitation from Prime Minister Yitzhak Rabin. As it turned out, I happened to be in Israel at the time and was able to meet him.

133

MEETING WITH GOLDA MEIR

From the airport, Billy was driven to downtown Tel Aviv for a meeting with an old friend, former Prime Minister Golda Meir. Mrs. Meir was living quietly in retirement, working on her papers and enjoying her grandchildren. As Billy and the quintessential Jewish grandmother embraced, I was reminded of a call I had received from T.W. Wilson just after the conclusion of the October 1973 Mideast War.

I was at a friend's house when T.W. reached me late one evening in early December. He said that Billy was in St. Louis, preparing for the start of a major crusade there, and wanted Mrs. Meir, who was meeting in Washington with President Nixon at the time, to address his crusade audience on Saturday night. Although Billy realized her presence might be interpreted as a political gesture, he wanted the prime minister, the people of Israel, and his worldwide constituency to know that he was solidly behind Israel in its continuing struggle for survival.

Late that night, through the efforts of Rabbi Marc Tannenbaum of the American Jewish Committee, Mrs. Meir was reached. She had to refuse the invitation because of a cabinet meeting, which was scheduled to take place early Sunday morning in Jerusalem. Graham, however, was so eager to talk personally and confidentially with the prime minister that he had a special telephone line installed in his St. Louis hotel suite. He then asked me to go to Washington to give Mrs. Meir that special phone number. And on Friday of that week, the day before her departure for Israel, the two friends had a long and valuable telephone conversation. Graham later told me that he had also talked by telephone with President Nixon three times during the October War, and reminded him on those occasions that the overwhelming number of evangelical Christians in the United States were firm supporters of Israel.

When they met that day in Tel Aviv, Mrs. Meir and Graham exhibited mutual esteem that was immediately apparent. During their time together that afternoon, the former prime minister delightedly autographed several copies of *My Life,* her recently published autobiography, for Billy. He told her about the book on angels that he had been working on. This prompted an interesting exchange on the subject of those curious beings, with Mrs. Meir demonstrating her keen knowledge of the Biblical background of angels.

During Billy's meeting with the former prime minister, Walter and Grady had been waiting in the car, but were ushered into the apartment when the meeting ended. Walter took a picture of Mrs. Meir autographing a copy of her book for Ruth Graham. Billy would later have the photo pasted in the book under Mrs. Meir's inscription. It was to be a special Christmas present for Ruth. A few days later, Billy remarked that *My Life* was "about the greatest book I have ever read."

A FASCINATING DRIVE

At 6:00, we were back in the Mercedes, and headed for Jerusalem. The car eased through the late afternoon traffic of Tel Aviv, a growing city in which new hotels and office buildings were constantly under construction. After passing through the suburbs and the network of industrial parks and kibbutzim, we suddenly came upon the wide expanse of the valley of Ajalon—the place where Joshua made the sun stand still. The view was breathtaking, and appeared even more beautiful against the setting sun. I believe this last part of the drive from Tel Aviv to Jerusalem must rate as one of the most fascinating in the world, especially for those who are interested in Biblical history.

Once past the valley, we entered the Bab al Wad, the narrow gorge located at the point of ascent to Jerusalem. It was in this ravine that a great deal of the decisive fighting in Israel's 1948 War of Independence had taken place. The sides of the road were still littered with burned-out military vehicles—vivid reminders of the destruction and sacrifice through which the modern Jewish nation had come into being.

From the Bab al Wad, the road continued to rise. Following a series of hairpin turns, the lights of Jerusalem finally came into view. Billy became as excited as any tourist who was seeing the city for the first time. He expressed how eager he was to discover what changes had occurred since his last visit.

The limousine turned onto Herzl Road and, within minutes, we were in the lobby of the Jerusalem Hilton. Although it was an unusually busy evening, the hotel manager, Peter Demopolis, greeted us immediately. In addition to Billy, there happened to be two other famous guests staying at the hotel—U.N. Secretary General Kurt Waldheim, who was on a swing through several regional capitals; and entertainer Frank Sinatra, who was in town for two benefit concerts.

Security in the hotel and its environs was tighter than usual. Only two weeks earlier, seven teenagers had been killed in a terrorist attack in central Jerusalem. The next day's busy schedule included a trip to Hadassah Hospital, where Billy planned to visit some of those who had been injured in the attack.

IN THE OLD CITY OF JERUSALEM

At 8:00 the next morning we were driven to the office of the city's dynamic mayor, Teddy Kolleck. Billy had known Kolleck for many years, and the two men greeted one another warmly. Kolleck was particularly interested in showing his visitor a major restoration project that was underway in the ancient Jewish quarter of the Old City of Jerusalem.

After some small talk and a discussion of local politics, Kolleck and his chief adviser, Yissachar Ben Yaacov, accompanied us on a tour. Our two-car caravan took us past the Avenue of the Paratroopers, the street that marked the pre-1967 border between Jordan and Israel. From there, we headed east through the Jaffa Gate and then down the narrow lane that led to the Jewish section of the Old City.

Kolleck directed the drivers to park in an area next to a newly constructed Yeshiva, and we began our walking tour toward the Western Wall—the focal point of Jewish religious and national life. As we walked, the mayor pointed out the ruins of several ancient synagogues, and called our attention to a series of archaeological excavations that were aimed at unearthing information about the Jewish past, particularly during the period from the return of the Jews from Babylon in 587 BC to the destruction of the Second Temple in 70 AD.

Graham was especially interested in matters concerning religious practice, so he questioned Ben Yaacov about the controversial dig in the Temple area, which had been the subject of a bitter dispute between the United Nations Educational, Scientific and Cultural Organization (UNESCO) and the Israeli government. Due to another dig near the Temple Mount, there was speculation that Israel planned to erect another temple. Billy had read as much in evangelical publications and wanted to know if there was any truth to the rumor. Mayor Kolleck quickly responded:

We have absolutely no interest in constructing another temple. We feel that the Western Wall itself is enough of a sacred place to provide a focus for Jewish spiritual observance. Also, we are very concerned with the care of the religious shrines of other faiths, and this area has important meaning for Moslems.

Kolleck's words referred to the Temple Mount, upon which the Dome of the Rock and the Al Aqsa Mosque stood. According to Islamic tradition, the Dome of the Rock contained the huge stone Abraham used in the sacrifice of his own son Isaac, while the Mosque was built upon the spot from which the prophet Mohammed ascended into heaven. The mayor said that he was aware that many evangelicals connected the rebuilding of the temple with the return of Christ. He insisted, however, that Israel would not contemplate such construction.

Our next stop was the Western Wall itself. By the time we arrived, it was a little after 11:00 and the broad plaza near the Wall was already filled with people. There were tourists, as well as Israelis who came from all parts of their country to observe or join those who were engaged in prayer at the Wall—the only remaining portion of the Second Temple. Graham appeared to be both intensely interested and moved by the massive stone structure, as well as the obvious sincerity of the worshippers.

Mayor Kolleck explained that when the Romans destroyed Jerusalem in 70 AD, they left this wall, which had actually formed the western part of a larger wall that once surrounded the outer courtyard of the Temple grounds. It had been left as a reminder to the Jews of the destruction of their nation. The mayor then commented that the Wall was a symbol of the survival of the Jewish people. As he spoke to us, his voice, which had been light and full of bounce just moments earlier, became solemn. For Teddy Kolleck, no visit to the Wall was a mundane experience. As he spoke, he was clearly caught up in the remembrance of the tragic history of the Jewish people and the miraculous renewal and rejuvenation that occurred with the creation of the Jewish State.

We were all touched by Kolleck's demeanor, and could almost feel his inner spiritual experience. As I listened to Kolleck at the Wall and at the other sites along our tour, I couldn't help but think that all major cities would benefit from having such an enthusiastic mayor as their champion.

Q. What is your favorite Bible verse?

A. *My favorite verse of Scripture was taught to me by my mother when I was just a little boy: "For God so loved the world, that He gave His only begotten Son, that whosoever believeth in Him should not perish, but have everlasting life."*

From the Wall, our group walked through the *souk*—the Arab market. For years, its narrow streets, which were lined with vendors selling their wares, have been a major center of interest to visitors of Jerusalem. I noted that even here, in an area 6,000 miles from America (and by no means a strong point of evangelical activity), Billy Graham was recognized, and people clamored for his autograph.

THE MOUNT OF OLIVES

After a fifteen-minute stroll through the market, we left the Old City through the Damascus Gate and returned to our cars. We then began our drive up the steep slope of the Mount of Olives. After passing through a bustling Arab hillside village, we arrived at the top of the mount, where stretched out beneath us was a breathtaking view of the Old City of Jerusalem we had just left. Mayor Kolleck told us that this view was most enchanting in the evening, when one could see the lights of Jerusalem and its surrounding suburbs almost as far as Bethlehem, the place of Jesus's birth.

The mayor called our attention to the Jewish cemetery located directly beneath the summit. He pointed out the many gravestones that were broken and destroyed during the period of Jordanian occupation prior to 1967. The broken markers were being repaired as part of a restoration project.

The Graham party was especially interested in the topography leading to Gethsemane, where Jesus had prayed during His last night on Earth. They asked about the route He had taken prior to His arrest. Kolleck gave us a running account of the path Jesus had likely traversed, and then pointed to the areas inside the city walls that had played important roles in His trial and crucifixion.

The panoramic view from the Mount of Olives gave Kolleck the opportunity to discuss the seizure and liberation of the Old City during the Six-Day War in June of 1967. He called our attention to the Golden Gate, which was sealed. According to Jewish tradition, this gate was not to be opened until the coming of the Messiah. Although that entrance would have afforded the Israeli troops their best route to the Old City and the Western Wall during the Six-Day War, they would not blow the gate open. Out of respect for age-old Jewish beliefs concerning the Golden Gate's Messianic significance, they attacked instead through Saint Stephen's Gate, causing them to sustain considerable loss of life among the paratroopers as they liberated the Old City.

Billy was engrossed with the mayor's account. And as I observed Billy, I thought about his interest in Israel. The movie

His Land, produced in 1970 by World Wide Pictures and filmed on location in Israel, offered a thorough evangelical theological perspective on the state, while conveying a sympathetic understanding of the reborn Jewish nation. The film, which would eventually be seen by more than 10 million people in the United States and Canada, demonstrated Billy's deep concern for the people of Israel. It also expressed an interest that went far beyond the spiritual dimension into the political arena, where Israel, then and now, struggled for its very existence.

The evening prior to Kolleck's tour, I had asked Billy how he was able to balance sympathy for Israel with concern for the status of Christians living in the Arab world. He had always been very careful to maintain his contacts with that group of believers. For example, during his visit to Cairo the previous week, he spent two days meeting privately with a delegation of Christians from conflict-torn Lebanon. He explained that his ministry was worldwide in scope, and he must never inhibit opportunities to minister, particularly in settings where local Christians were troubled and seeking his presence and message.

VISIT WITH YITZHAK RABIN

The next stop on Graham's itinerary was the residence of Israel's Prime Minister Yitzhak Rabin, who had planned a luncheon in Billy's honor. There, Billy was graciously welcomed at the door by the prime minister's wife, Leah. Within a few moments, Rabin emerged from a small study and warmly greeted the evangelist and his associates.

Rabin and Graham had met on several occasions during the years when the former chief of staff of the Israel Defense Forces served as Israel's ambassador to the United States. I had the opportunity to speak with Rabin a few days before Graham's visit and was impressed both with his grasp of the nuances of American religious life, and his specific interest in the activities of evangelical Christians. Rabin told me he had appeared many times before church groups while serving as ambassador. He said that he had come away believing that evangelicals comprised much of Israel's non-Jewish support in the United States.

The prime minister had invited a cross section of religious leaders, government officials, and representatives of the foreign ministry to attend the luncheon. One of the guests, Dr. M. Bernard Reznikoff of the American Jewish Committee, was responsible for the distribution in Israel of *His Land*. He asked Billy to give his regards to several World Wide Pictures executives with whom he had worked. Billy, Grady, and Walter were especially pleased to see their old friend Bob Lindsay at the luncheon. Bob was a Southern Baptist official who was stationed in Israel and had lost a leg during the 1948 War of Independence.

After lunch, many of the guests questioned Billy concerning Biblical prophecy and the role of Israel in Christian eschatology. They were also interested in learning Billy's views on the future of Israel, to which Billy replied that he believed the establishment of Israel as a state was a forerunning event connected with the return of Christ to Earth. He went on to explain his interpretation of the Biblical position regarding the Second Coming of Christ. A lively theological discussion ensued.

When the luncheon ended, Billy and Prime Minister Rabin went into another room for a private conversation. When they emerged, Billy said, "You know, when you visited me in my Washington hotel room a few years ago, I didn't realize that one day you would be Prime Minister Rabin." Rabin, not exactly known for expressions of levity, smiled and replied, "Neither did I."

VISITING THE WOUNDED

The last stop on Graham's schedule was Hadassah Hospital. Billy's main purpose in visiting the huge ultramodern facility was to spend some time with the victims of a recent terrorist attack.

Upon his arrival, Billy was met by one of the hospital administrators, who took him directly to the wards that housed the injured. Several of the patients were in desperate condition. Billy had much experience ministering to wounded American troops in both the Korean and Vietnam wars, and he spoke patiently and comfortably with many of the patients that afternoon. There was a man who had been blinded and was not expected to survive. Another patient, who had miraculously survived the full force of the bombing, showed Billy some pieces of shrapnel that had been taken from his head. And another patient, whose entire body was covered in bandages, somehow managed—in spite of his obvious pain—to shake Graham's hand and thank him for coming.

Before leaving, we visited the hospital synagogue, which housed the famous Chagall Windows—magnificent stained glass depictions of the Twelve Tribes of Israel. The group was quite impressed by the beauty and intricate design of each framed window, and Billy, who was always very eager to gain knowledge on new and challenging subjects, asked a number of questions concerning Chagall's technique and the composition of the materials used in creating the windows. Several days later, while he was in Paris, Graham came across an article on Chagall, which he immediately put into a file for future reading.

THE END OF THE DAY

Although the scheduled portion of Graham's day ended with his visit to the hospital, he still had some important work to do before turning in for the night. Back in his room at the Hilton, he worked on the text for an *Hour of Decision* broadcast. He then recorded the message with the aid of a technician who had been sent over from the Israel Broadcasting Authority.

When the recording session ended, a copy of the tape was forwarded to Cliff Barrows at his home studio in Greenville, South Carolina. In an emergency, Cliff was always able to dip into his well-stocked library of Billy's crusade messages to broadcast a substitute sermon on the *Hour of Decision*. Whenever possible, however, Billy liked to keep his messages as current as possible. The one he taped in Jerusalem would be aired around the world within three weeks.

10

"Now Is the Hour"

By 7:15, LONG LINES WERE FORMING at the stadium entrances. Buses pulled into the parking lot at the rate of six per minute, and out on Interstate 55, a stalled car blocked the lane leading to the stadium exit. Outside the south gates, five picketers solemnly distributed leaflets claiming "Billy Graham is a captive of modernism." For the most part, however, the incoming crowd was good humored. There were jokes about the impending rain being "real Baptist weather tonight." People courteously allowed others to scamper ahead of them up the concrete steps to the wooden grandstands.

Graham, accompanied by Grady and T.W., left the trailer and walked into the tunnel under the stands. Inside, they quickly passed an office and a small storeroom before entering the dressing room that was the staging point for the platform guests. The evangelist appeared quite relaxed as he stopped to chat with each of the men and women in the room. As he completed his circuit of the cramped space, he raised his voice in a brief prayer, saying, "God bless all of you for coming. We are going to have some rain tonight, but the Lord is in control, and we will give Him the glory and the honor."

Billy left the tunnel and entered the infield, where he was quickly spotted. His presence generated a wave of excitement as he made his way toward the platform. When Billy took his seat, Cliff Barrows stepped to the lectern and began the service. I eagerly watched from my seat in the press section.

After Cliff welcomed the crowd, which was still filtering into the stadium, the choir sang the stirring hymn, "Great Is Thy Faithfulness." Then the crusade prayer chairman, Mrs. Florence Greentree, presented the pastor of a large downtown church, who asked God to "Bless Your servant Billy Graham, and hold off the rain if it be in accordance with Your divine will." Cliff then sprang from his seat and introduced America's beloved gospel singer, George Beverly Shea, who sang "I'd Rather Have Jesus."

After he had made a few more announcements and the choir sang another hymn, Cliff introduced Billy Graham. The evangelist walked to the lectern and greeted the people in the audience before asking them to observe a moment of silent prayer for a person who had just become ill. When he broke the silence, Billy spoke of a "great black leader, a man originally from Mississippi, now pastor in a northern state, who came to visit me yesterday and who told me, 'You know, I would rather live in Mississippi than any state in the North,' and I think that says something about Mississippi." The audience responded with enthusiastic applause. Then Billy continued, "The people of Mississippi are generous, warm and friendly," and noted that, "We are in the stadium in which Ole Miss plays."

When the applause quieted, Graham became very serious. He spoke of the attack on the *Mayaguez*, which had been fired upon and seized in the Gulf of Siam, about sixty miles from the Cambodian coast. The crew had been captured. Graham asked, "What will the American response be?" He paused and then continued:

> These things are happening all over the world, and the Scriptures say there will come a day when the weak will say, "I'm strong," and those little nations will twist our tail and kick us and beat us, and there is nothing we can do about it—and we've already reached that stage. I'm glad I'm not president. I tell you, something would be done about it!

Just as the audience began to applaud, the rain started to fall. People began reaching for their umbrellas; Grady placed Billy's tan raincoat on his chair. The temporary canopy that had been placed over the stage helped provide cover from the rain.

THE OFFERING

Billy then announced to the crowd, which had settled under a sea of opened umbrellas, that the offering was about to be received. He also indicated that the proceeds would be going to his organization's Emergency Relief Fund. In an effort to explain something of the fund's purpose, he said:

Did you know that the world right now is probably on the verge of the greatest famine in the history of mankind? Right now, at this moment, 10,000 people a day are starving for lack of food. In some parts of Africa, I read the other day, they have eaten everything they can lay their hands on—cats, dogs, mice, birds, bark off the trees, manure, and, in some cases, even each other—just to stay alive.

We in America are 6 percent of the world's population, but we consume 50 percent of the world's goods. A food conference in Rome was told there's only one problem in the world today—not two problems, not three, just one—the question of feeding the world's huge population. One third of the world is well fed; one third of the world is starving. The Rome conference said the human race stands at the greatest crisis of its existence, and it's very doubtful that we can survive as a human race.

And Jesus said that you and I as Christians have a responsibility: "I was hungry and you gave me food, and I was thirsty and you gave me drink." Have you been doing that? Our association, which is called the Billy Graham Evangelistic Association, has set up an Emergency Relief Fund, and if you want to send money to us and earmark it for that, we'll see that it gets to the people. We will guarantee that 90 percent of it gets there; 10 percent has to be kept out by different agencies and so forth, for the transportation, and all the rest of it; but when we write a check to someplace in Africa, or some agency, we put on that check, "Given in the name of the Lord Jesus Christ." We believe that we have a responsibility to those who are hungry, and especially to those fellow believers in other parts of the world who are suffering.

Then ushers circulated through the stands, passing out cardboard pails into which the offerings were placed. It appeared that nearly everybody contributed, and the donations were largely bills, rather than small change.

THE "MAN IN BLACK"

When the choir had completed its song, Billy once again turned to the audience. He thanked them for their generosity, and then, with a smile, announced:

> Tonight, I do not need to introduce our special guest because he's known all over America and all over the world. All you have to do is talk about the "Man in Black"—and he's talking about it in a brand new book that he's written, a spiritual autobiography that I know is going to be a bestseller. My wife and I are planning to buy copies and give them away as Christmas presents this year because we believe in this couple. Tonight, I am proud and honored and thrilled and flattered to present my very good and warm friend in Christ, Johnny Cash.

As Cash and his troupe made their way to the front of the platform, the red light on the television camera began to flash, signifying that this part of the program was being recorded. In addition to Cash, the camera would also record a hymn sung by Bev Shea, Billy's sermon, and the invitation at the conclusion of the service.

The order of the program was standard with all of the Graham crusades. It was a successful formula that the organization had established long ago. When I asked a team member why this format had seen little innovation over the years, he responded, "Like everyone else, Graham falls into a certain pattern—he has discovered what works for him and there is little need for change."

After greeting his friends on stage, Billy returned to his seat, while Johnny Cash and June Carter stood next to the podium. While they were in Jackson to sing, they also wanted to speak to the crusade audience. Cash began by saying:

> Thank you, Billy, for those kind words. June and I appreciate them very much. *Man in Black,* as he said, is an autobiography, a spiritual autobiography. I told him just before the service tonight that I'm glad to say that the spiritual autobiography is very incomplete, because we have a lot that we're trying to learn and a lot that we're still trying to do. It was almost eight years ago that we renewed our total commitment to Jesus Christ and I just wanted to say, in case anybody had any doubt, that I'm a Christian and I'm awfully proud to say so.

Cash and company then performed "The Ragged Old Flag." At the conclusion of the song, Johnny turned once again to the audience and said, "Ladies and gentlemen, here is my right arm, the woman in my life, and the sweetest thing I've ever known— my wife, June Carter." Turning to acknowledge Johnny's tribute, June Carter said, "That's the most wonderful belated Mother's Day present that a woman could hear. Bless your heart." She continued:

> I would like to say praise the Lord for that ragged old flag, and for that ragged old husband of mine. You know, we have so much to be thankful for, and I stop daily to count my bless- ings. But tonight, I was thinking as he sang "The Ragged Old Flag," how much we truly have to be thankful for in these United States of America. To have the ragged old flag hanging there is fine, and the greatest blessing is that you can have Jesus Christ in your heart, because that's where He lives within me—in my heart. And, I'm proud to say, as a mother and wife, He lives in the heart of my family as well. Billy, thank you for inviting us. We're so glad to be with you, so glad to be a part of this great crusade here in Jackson, Mississippi.

Johnny Cash and June Carter took their seats on the platform next to Billy, while the musicians returned to their seats along the running track at the side of the stage.

THE MESSAGE

The rain continued to fall in steady, slanting sheets, and the platform's protective canopy began filling with water. Bev Shea, wearing a plastic slicker, stepped to the center of the stage and sang the great crusade favorite "How Great Thou Art." The cold cascading rain did nothing to dampen Shea's spirit or the power of his inspirational voice.

At the conclusion of the hymn, Billy, who had put on his raincoat, stood at the podium with his Bible in hand. As the canopy only partially protected him from the rain, a committee member held an umbrella over his head as he gave his sermon. It was the crusade's Youth Night, and Billy chose to begin his message by reading Mark 10:17–22, the story of the rich young man who came to Jesus seeking eternal life. It was one of the *New Testament's* most familiar passages.

Now there are many things I would like to say about this passage tonight. It's the story of a young aristocrat coming to Jesus Christ—handsome, we can suppose, certainly wealthy, and young. But he was like thousands of young people and older people alike here tonight. He was seeking something else in life. He wasn't satisfied with the way life was at the moment. The pressures of life were too great. He might have been a university student, he might have been a senior student. I don't know. But right now, we have a phenomenon that's been sweeping America for about eight years: younger people have suddenly become interested in religion once again. For a while it was the middle-aged—it was my generation that seemed to be interested. Now my generation became more materialistic and secularistic, and it has been young people coming along that have talked of spiritual things and talked about God. Some of them are looking in the wrong place. Some of them are looking in the Eastern religions; some of them are looking in the occult. But thousands of them have been turning to Jesus Christ.

Now as I look on young people today, I want to bring up a number of things that I see among you young people—and I'm old enough to say "you young people." I'm fifty-six years old, if you want to know my age. I have five children and nine grandchildren, and two on the way. So tonight, I want you to see yourselves the way I see you.

First, I believe there is a breakdown of home life, and it has led to a moral and spiritual void. Even in some of the finest Christian homes, the God has become television. That little set we gather around—the only time the family is quiet, the only time the family has any little reverence is around that set. It used to be around the family Bible; it used to be around God; it used to be around prayer. But now, about the only time you can get the family together is if they agree on a certain program. And if they don't, most homes now have two sets, so you divide the family. But there is a spiritual void, and when you think of one out of every two or three marriages breaking up, you have millions of young people being thrown out without the roots of a father and mother at home. And then, in the homes that stay together, many times you have a lack of love between parents, and the young people are affected psychologically and spiritually.

I also find there is a tremendous dissatisfaction among young people with their lives as they are. A young person told me just the other day, "I don't know what's wrong. I've got everything. I am a senior at the university, but," he said, "I'm just dissatisfied with myself." I said, "Do you know why? Everybody has this same type of dissatisfaction until they find Jesus Christ."

I find in this generation of young people that sexual relationships don't provide the emotional closeness they thought they would. They are not finding the peace and happiness and the kicks and the deep satisfaction they thought they would find in all the so-called sex freedom. It has brought about a whole new set of psychological problems that affect them the rest of their lives, especially their future marriage.

And I find tremendous loneliness among young people.

They can have friends, they can be in a crowd, but there is also loneliness. You know why? You're lonely for God. You were made for God. You were made in God's image and you are lonely for Him and don't know it. We had one of the great psychiatrists of the country here the other night, and he said to me, when he came into my little trailer, that one of the great problems he has to deal with in his great psychiatric clinic is the problem of loneliness on the part of young people. Jesus can be closer than a brother; He can settle that loneliness. You see, you were made for God, for fellowship with God. And without God, there is loneliness. Give your life to Christ tonight and never know another lonely moment.

I find restlessness among young people. They're very restless. Now, a certain amount of restlessness during a teenage period is normal—I've had five teenage children and they were all restless. From a parent's point of view, they just had more energy than we had; that was really the problem. There's another kind of deeper restlessness that I'm talking about. I'm not talking about just getting up and running around and jumping around and riding a motorcycle and all those things—that comes with being a teenager. But there is restlessness where they don't find peace and rest until they come to know Christ in a personal way.

There is also a feeling of emptiness and purposelessness. They haven't found purpose and meaning in their lives, so they are empty and they are bored. Let Christ come into your heart and fill that emptiness and take that boredom away.

I find that many young people are despondent. They despair easily. They get discouraged, they get down-in-the-dumps, they have depressions, and many of them are going to see psychiatrists and psychologists and clergy, trying to get something to pick them up. And a great many prescriptions today are being given to young people that need a little pickup.

And then I find that for this generation of young people, it's almost impossible for them to make decisions—about vocation, marriage, moral values, if there is a moral code or a moral absolute to make a decision about.

I find that young people feel a sense of guilt, and they

don't know why. But it's there and it causes all kinds of psychological problems. Well, of course, we are guilty; we have broken God's law. There is a psychological guilt that's wrong. But there's a right kind of guilt, in which you are guilty before God of breaking God's law, and that's called sin. And it needs to be repented of, and it needs to be brought back to the cross, and then don't let the devil put that guilt back on you. When you are forgiven by God, you are forgiven. And God not only forgives, He forgets. And when you are justified in the sight of God, that means just as though you have never sinned. Come to Christ tonight; let Him take that guilt away.

Finally, I find that disillusionment is beginning to grow. I'm delighted at this, and I hope I'm right. I read it in one of the magazines—our disillusionment with drugs as the answer to the problems that young people were using five or six or seven or eight years ago, when they thought that LSD and all the rest were the ultimate of experiences. And now they are beginning to be educated to the fact that this is destructive.

Now, when you come to Jesus, I want to tell you something: In one way, there is a high; but that's very dangerous, because when you come to Christ, it is not always living on a high. There are periods when you will get discouraged, just like other people. But that doesn't mean that you have lost Christ.

There are two men in the *Old Testament*—two of the greatest men—that said, "God kill me." Moses said, "These people are too much for me, Lord; just kill me now." And Elijah said, "Lord, slay me; Jezabel is after me." And you know, the Lord came and ministered to both of them. God understands when you get discouraged. You see, we're giving a false teaching if we teach that you come to Christ and you're always on top. Life isn't that way. Read the Psalmist.

But let me tell you, your highs become more permanent, and the highs are much longer lasting and much deeper and much greater, and after you have learned the ways of God, and you've learned to walk with the Lord, it becomes a wonderful, thrilling life. Problems? Yes. Persecution? Yes. Misunderstanding? Yes. That all goes with taking your stand for Christ and it's all part of discipline.

Now what about you? I think that many of you are like this young man; you've been searching for something. This young man might not have known exactly what he was searching for. He said, "Lord, I want eternal life." By "eternal life," he meant: "I want to have a successful life here and now." I don't mean material prosperity; he already had that. I mean a successful inner life. The second thing he meant was, "I want eternal life in the sense of the future; I want to know that when I die, I'm going to heaven."

Billy Graham was thirty minutes into his message, and there was hardly any movement in the stadium. Even the pouring rain didn't appear to bother the crowd as they listened in rapt attention to the evangelist. In this and in all of Billy's sermons, he quoted quite liberally from the Scriptures. The large black Bible he favored in the pulpit was clearly visible in his hand from time to time as he punctuated his language and imagery with an outstretched left arm.

Harold Lindsell's analysis of Billy's pulpit style came to mind as I watched the evangelist speak that night. Lindsell had said, "He falls in line generally with the great evangelists of the ages. If you read the sermons of Charles Haddon Spurgeon, you will not find contemporaneity. Jonathan Edwards would speak only in contemporary terms about his congregants' sin. Moody always preached in a Biblical context, as did Charles E. Fuller. Billy has been more interested in contemporary events," Lindsell observed, "But his preaching is based on two convictions. First, the word of God has power and will not return void; and, second, the Holy Spirit prepares the listener for an encounter with Christ through the word."

I shifted my attention back to the platform, where, despite the rain, Graham continued his message about the young rich man:

He came with urgency, he ran to Jesus. There was an urgency about it. And there is an urgency about you. I'll tell you why. We don't know what day tomorrow is going to be. The Bible says remember the Creator in the days of our youth. But there is a different urgency in our generation. Our America, this country, and the world are changing more rapidly than at any time in the history of the whole human race since the days of Noah—and it changed rapidly in those days; in forty days and forty nights it was wiped out.

We've got the ability now to wipe ourselves out for the first time since the flood. There are many nations working on the atomic bomb—you are going to see things that are going to tear the human race apart. You're going to have to live through it or die in it. I hope that isn't true, but I think it's going to be true.

The Bible teaches us that antiChrist, or the spirit of anti-Christ, is everywhere. There's an urgency about coming to Christ. Come to Christ while you can. There's an urgency because of this crusade. Did you know that I was asked by a newspaper reporter tonight when I thought we'd be back in Jackson for another crusade? I said, "Well, the next time, I'll probably have to be rolled up in a wheelchair." When will we ever see a crowd like this, in a stadium like this again in Jackson? Maybe never. Thousands have prayed and thousands have worked and thousands have given; and God has prepared your heart, and God has spoken to you, and you know that you have to make a commitment to Christ. The Bible says My spirit shall not always strive for man. Unless God, the Holy Spirit, makes you uncomfortable and brings you and draws you, you can't come to Christ. And He's doing that tonight in this meeting.

And then that rich man had the right attitude of humility. He didn't come up to Christ with his shoulders back and say, "Look what a great guy I am." He fell down before Christ and said, "Lord, I know there's something wrong with my life. I need something else. I want eternal life." That was an amazing sight—this rich young aristocrat falling at the feet of the penniless prophet of Nazareth, who was on His way to being an outlaw, and who was going to be crucified in a short time as a common criminal. But this young man didn't care who saw. He came in the open, publicly, to Christ, and he asked the right question. What did he ask? He said, "What must I do?"

Psychology Today, a magazine for psychologists, polled its readership recently and asked what they wanted more than anything in the world. We had a girl last night who sang. Most of you don't know who she was. But she's been written up in some magazines and papers, and it's been speculated that she's the richest woman in the world since the death of her father. I don't know whether that's true or not. I've never discussed money with her. She was here because she is a dynamic Christian. She was here because she has a beautiful voice, and she's dedicated to Christ.

What would you rather have more than anything in the whole world? "Oh, boy, if I could just get my hands on a million bucks!" Or, "If I could get that girl to say yes that I've been chasing."

No. Eternal life. In the survey that *Psychology Today* made, they said the thing they wanted more than anything in the world is eternal life. If you have eternal life, you have everything. You know that little ad on television—If you have your health, you have just about everything? Well, I want to tell you, if you don't have spiritual health and you don't have Christ, you haven't got anything, because this body is going to die. This brain is going to stop some day; this heart is going to stop some day.

We need eternal life, and eternal life is provided by the Lord, Jesus Christ. He can give you eternal life tonight, now. You don't have to wait until you die to get eternal life, you can get it right now. I want you to get out of your seat and come right now and receive Christ.

I was surprised at the rapid transition from sermon to invitation. As Billy spoke the words, there was a definite air of expectancy among the attendees, most of whom were familiar with the crusade pattern. They knew that Graham would conclude with the invitation, and they were prepared to hear him make the offer of salvation through personal commitment to Christ.

As soon as Graham said, "I want you to get out of your seat . . ." some of those in the audience got up and started to walk toward the infield. Then, within only a few minutes, a re-markable number of people left their seats and made their way toward the platform.

COMING FORWARD IN THE RAIN

The rain, which had been heavy and chilling, suddenly became a downpour, but it didn't stop the steady flow of people from head-ing toward the stage. Even those who remained in their seats seemed to sense the high drama and derive vicarious pleasure in watching the multitude come forward. Then, as a growing num-ber of people gathered near Billy, he spoke to them from the stage, asking them to pray with him. A few minutes later, Graham turned toward the television camera and tendered a special invi-tation to his viewing audience, saying, "Hundreds of people are coming forward tonight in Jackson, Mississippi. Won't you come to Christ now? There may never be a better opportunity than now to give your life to Christ." Then, looking out into the stands, Gra-ham asked others to come forward:

> God may be working on your heart. The Bible says, "Now is the day of salvation, this is the accepted time." I want you to leave your seats and come down here in front of the platform and join these people who have decided to make Jesus Christ their personal Lord and Savior. Your friends will wait for you. If you've come by bus, the bus will wait. I want you to come and accept Christ as Lord.

Unlike many other evangelists, Graham did not plead, cajole, or beg. His invitation was low key, but there was little doubt of his earnestness.

From where I was sitting, I spotted Grady Wilson, who was studying the crowd from his seat on the platform. From his face and the faces of the team members who were circulating through-out the infield, I sensed that something extraordinary was occur-ring. All of the telephone calls, letters, meetings, appointments, offerings, airplane trips, miles of travel, and weeks away from family and everyday preoccupations had come down to the wrestling for souls that was now going on. There, in a thirty-by-thirty-yard square, counselors and inquirers were grappling with issues of greater significance than the *Mayaguez*, or integration, or the anticipated price of cotton.

Most of those who came down from the stands at Graham's invitation were experiencing a moment of truth. They were making a crucial decision, committing themselves in a way that would shape their thoughts, habits, and, perhaps, their destinies. Whether it was the result of God, the words of Billy Graham, a childhood memory brought to the surface by a prayer, or the sense of community felt by sitting in an arena with thousands of other people, these inquirers had been moved to rise from their seats. They placed themselves in an existential situation in which they were ready to acknowledge their inadequacy, sinfulness, and need.

Q. What kind of music do you like?

A. *I like mood music when studying. I listen to a lot of Christian music. My favorite artists are George Beverly Shea and Sandi Patti. I love to hear the old songs like "Harvest Moon." I like to hear quiet music, and I like to hear good symphony orchestras and Strauss waltzes.*

I got up from my seat and walked among the inquirers. As I made my way through the crowd, I understood what Graham's associate Sherwood Wirt had said to me before we left for the stadium: "There is nothing going on in the world like what you will see out there tonight." Everywhere I looked, people were talking to each other. A female counselor in a wheelchair spoke to a woman who was committing herself to Christ; a young white woman talked with a black teenager, promising to call her the next morning; a heavy-set black pastor conversed with a well-dressed young white man; two Marines in dress whites were being counseled by an Air Force corporal; five elderly patients from a Veterans Administration hospital listened somberly to a counselor; and Judy Butler, Charlie Riggs's secretary, led a young girl from the county reformatory to Christ.

Later, with the assistance of Roger Palm of *Decision* magazine, I would learn of many others who had responded to Billy's invitation. There was the three-year-old girl who had asked her parents to take her forward; a church deacon who told his counselor, "The hardest thing for me is that I am going to have to tell my pastor and fellow deacons that I've been living a hypocritical life all these years"; and the husband and wife who, as the result of a traffic jam on I-55, changed their initial plans, unexpectedly attended the rally, and then came forward together. I also learned of the fifteen-year-old boy who walked on crutches from the stadium's top tier to get to the infield; the manufacturing executive who removed a gold Playboy Club card from his wallet, saying, "I won't be needing this any more"; and the young man with a speech problem who came forward only to discover that his counselor was a speech therapist.

SPEAKING WITH THE INQUIRERS

One did not have to be a believer to sense the drama of what was happening on the infield. I truly hoped that those who had come forward would be experiencing positive and enduring changes in their lives, and that they would gain a more solid foundation in coping with life's difficulties and disappointments.

I was struck by the large number of blacks—and particularly the black teenagers—who responded to Billy's invitation. Jim Pearson, a local pastor, looked across the field and said, "The number of blacks coming forward is very encouraging to those of us who want to see things in Mississippi on an equal footing between the races, in the sight of man as well as in the sight of God."

I was also keenly interested in what prompted a person's decision to come forward. I wished I could have talked to all of the inquirers who stood in the infield that evening. I did, however, manage to speak with a number of those who had accepted Graham's invitation.

Brother and Sister

Thirteen-year-old Jimmy Wheatly came to the crusade with his fifteen-year-old sister Sue, who had accepted Christ at a summer camp the year before. Jimmy, an officer in the Training Union of his Baptist Church, attended church and Sunday school for as long as he could remember. Until that night in Jackson, however, he had never made a commitment to Christ.

Sue had been praying very earnestly for her brother to respond to the invitation that night; but when it was extended, Jimmy stayed put. He seemed distracted, and Sue worried that he wasn't going to go forward. From their seats high in the stands, the siblings watched people walk toward the platform as the choir sang the revival hymn "Just As I Am." Sue suddenly turned to her brother and asked him outright if he wanted to come to Christ. He responded by saying, "Yes," and then asked Sue if she would accompany him to the infield. Sue was more than happy to comply, and the two descended the concrete stairway arm in arm.

They Weren't Talking, But . . .

Tom and Ellen Bryant were not church members, but they had come to the crusade as a favor to the Cushings, their next-door neighbors. Laura Cushing had been active in the crusade's prayer campaign, and Ellen had attended one of the prayer sessions in Laura's home.

The Bryants were a young couple in their late twenties, and had been living in Jackson only a few months. Ellen was very unhappy about the relocation, which came about when Tom left his job in northern Virginia to take a position with a bank in Jackson. Ellen hadn't wanted her husband to take the new job because it meant moving away from her family and close friends. She was very lonely and depressed, and the stress was creating trouble within their marriage.

When they arrived at the service, the Bryants were barely talking to each other. Tom had had a busy day, and wasn't in the mood to attend the meeting. To make matters worse, Ellen had arranged for them to drive to the stadium with the Cushings. As Larry Cushing was a counselor, this meant they wouldn't be able to leave until Larry had completed his duties for the evening. The heavy downpour contributed to Tom's gloomy mood, and by the time Billy's message began, Tom was cursing under his breath. Even the sermon seemed off-key—Billy spoke to teens and Tom couldn't relate. Ellen tried to follow the sermon, but was preoccupied with Tom's mood and the problems they were having.

When the message ended and Billy made his invitation, the Bryants—although there was no logical reason why they did so—rose and walked hand in hand to the front of the platform. There, they were met and counseled by the pastor of a Pentecostal church. After twenty minutes of conversation, prayer, and lots of tears, Tom and Ellen Bryant made decisions for Christ.

When I asked the young couple what had brought them forward, Ellen could only say that it was out of their sense of despondency. Somehow, Ellen said, change seemed to be possible, but they had to reach out and grasp it.

He Had a Drinking Problem

A native of a small Delta town, Bill Franklin, a fifty-three-year-old widower, lived in Jackson most of his adult life. For the past several months, Bill, who was a mailman, found himself delivering a considerable number of letters that had been marked with the return address "Billy Graham Mississippi Crusade." Although it had been years since Bill had been in a church, the Mississippi Crusade envelopes piqued his curiosity, and explained his presence at the evening's service.

Bill had been addicted to alcohol for the past fifteen years. Although he tried to limit his heavy drinking to weekends and vacations, occasionally he had to take a day or two off work to recover from an alcoholic stupor.

Bill arrived at the stadium early, took a seat in the end zone, and found himself looking forward to the evening program. Bill liked the singing—it reminded him of the little church he used to attend as a child. He tried to pay attention to the sermon, but the rain and chill bothered him a great deal. Then, toward the end of the message, he heard Billy say how one can be certain of eternal life. From that point, Bill followed the evangelist's every word.

When the invitation was given, Bill was one of the first people to head for the platform area, where the proprietor of a hardware store met and counseled him. Bill was very concerned about his drinking problem; he asked the counselor if Graham's words about all things becoming new when a man accepted Christ were accurate. Assured that committing to Christ would make him into a new man, Bill prayed with his counselor, who promised to telephone him the next evening.

Sense of Sin

Eighteen-year-old Sarah Herndon arrived at the stadium after a long and tiring day. A cashier at a local supermarket, Sarah had made several mistakes at work that day, prompting angry stares from Mr. Johnson, the store manager. The past few weeks had been particularly difficult for Sarah. Three months earlier, she had given birth out of wedlock to a baby girl, who had been adopted by a couple in Georgia. Sarah had not been able to get over her sense of loss and desolation.

Until eighteen months earlier, Sarah had been an active church member and often listened to Billy Graham on the radio. Then, she met and fell in love with a student at Mississippi State. They lived together for several months, but when Sarah became pregnant, the boy refused to have anything more to do with her. Afraid to tell her father, and too ashamed to ask anyone for help, Sarah moved out of her house and into a small one-room apartment. She managed to scrape by for a while on the earnings from her supermarket job. When Sarah's father eventually discovered her condition, he made sure she received the proper medical care, and persuaded her to offer the baby for adoption.

After giving up her daughter, Sarah felt a deep sense of sin. She had come to the service hoping to find forgiveness; yet, she remained seated for quite some time after Graham had extended the invitation to come forward. Then Billy said, "There is someone here who needs to come forward, but is holding back. God is talking to you, and I want you to come." Sarah sensed that Billy was talking to her, and suddenly, it became easy to get up from her seat and move toward the infield.

Whites Only?

Sometimes medical skill and advanced technology are not enough to save a life during an emergency. Linda Mae Rogers, a nurse for fourteen years, had been monitoring the vital signs of a heart attack victim earlier in the day. After being in stable condition during the morning, the patient suffered another infarction, and at 4:15 in the afternoon, he died. Linda was used to death; however, sometimes she worked so hard to pull a patient through that she felt a personal sense of loss if the person died. Linda felt it with this patient—a white man who had never before come into close contact with a black person until he found himself under her care in the hospital emergency room.

Linda's religious background was nominal. Her parents were members of an AME congregation, but she and her husband, Fred, weren't really interested in going to church. As for the crusade, although it had piqued her interest because of all of the media attention it had received, Linda suspected that Graham would be speaking only to whites. As it turned out, on day four of the crusade, Linda's husband was in Memphis on an overnight trip. So when her shift ended, Linda, who was feeling somewhat down after the death of her patient, decided to drive over to the stadium. When she arrived, she took notice of the crowd and the choir, and was surprised at the number of blacks in attendance. She wondered if some of them had come out of curiosity or because they felt a sense of association and belonging.

Linda found Billy's sermon very convincing—not that she

believed herself to be guilty of any major sin, but because of what the evangelist said about a person's need for salvation; it seemed to make sense. And so, when the invitation was issued, she made the decision to come forward.

BACK AT THE TRAILER

When Billy concluded his remarks to the inquirers, he bade the audience good night and returned to the trailer, where he relaxed and waited for the crowd to disperse. Even so, many attendees stood near his car, hoping to talk with him, or at least see him.

As it happened, Billy's fashionably longish hair needed a trimming, so arrangements had been made by a local Methodist pastor to meet Billy back at the trailer with a barber. As the two men walked in the door, the pastor took Billy aside and told him, "This man is under the conviction of the Holy Spirit. I believe he is ready to receive Christ."

As the barber deftly wielded his comb and scissors, Billy spoke with him. He asked about his background. Was he married? How many children did he have? Was he a Christian? When the barber replied to this last question, he said that he wasn't sure if he was a Christian—that he had never made a definite commitment to Christ. Billy then asked if he would like to do so now.

"Yes," the barber responded, "I want Christ as my Savior."

And so this evangelist, who, over the years, had inspired multitudes to make decisions for Christ, and who, just moments earlier, had spoken words that moved many hundreds of people to come forward, patiently guided one more man to Christ. Billy Graham was a soul winner—it was his *raison d'être*.

11

The End of a Very Long Day

GRAHAM PLACED A CALL TO THE Municipal Airport from his trailer and reached Johnny Cash just as he and June Carter were about to board their private jet for the return trip to Nashville. He thanked Cash for appearing at the service, and then said a brief goodbye to June.

Grady came into the trailer and announced that soon they would be heading over to Jim Carr's home for that late-night dinner party. So Billy, Grady, and T.W. left the field and headed back to the Holiday Inn to freshen up before going to Jim's. On the drive back to the hotel, Billy suddenly became disconcerted when he discovered he couldn't find his large-print pulpit Bible. T.W. immediately radioed Don Bailey, and asked him to look for it on the platform. Don, who was already halfway to the Hilton with a full car of staff members, continued on to the hotel, dropped off his passengers, and returned to the stadium.

When Don got back to the stadium, he found Charlie Riggs standing in the driving rain with a black teenager. The youth had come forward that evening, but he had some serious personal problems and wanted to talk to Billy. Charlie was telling the young man that Billy had already left the stadium; but he took the boy's name and phone number, and promised to try to set up an appointment for him with the evangelist.

Riggs and Bailey then began their futile search of the platform for Billy's Bible. As they walked back to Don's car, they passed the grandstand, where a stunned father asked them where to pick up his daughter, who was lost. After directing him to the security office, the two colleagues looked at each other and shook their heads—it had been a very long day. Perhaps they would be able to enjoy a bit of relaxation and fellowship at the Carrs' home in a little while. When they reached Don's car, T.W. was on the radio, letting them know that Grady had found the missing Bible under the back seat of the Pontiac. As the last cars drove from the parking lot, the stadium electrician began cutting off the floodlights. There was, however, more work to be done that night.

FOLLOW-UP AT THE CO-LABOR STATION

In the nearby Mississippi Armory, the 200 people that made up the Jackson Crusade's Co-Labor crew began their four-hour shift. These workers compiled and organized the contact information on the cards that had been filled out by the 852 attendees who had come forward during the evening service. This follow-up work would help those who had made decisions for Christ connect with local churches and continue to grow in their Christian commitment.

The workers were seated at several aluminum folding tables. Some collated the personal information cards that had been completed by the counselors; others made several copies of each card—one copy remained with the crusade committee, another was forwarded to Graham headquarters, and the third was mailed immediately either to the inquirer's pastor or to a minister whose congregation was located near the inquirer's neighborhood.

The room was noisy, busy, and swelteringly hot. Messengers traversed the work area, picking up completed forms. One young man who could barely read or write, helped by passing out hamburgers and sodas. When the workers were about halfway through their appointed jobs, Cliff Barrows and television star Jerry Clower stopped by the armory to greet them. Clower, who had appeared at the service the previous evening, had been given a standing ovation by his fellow Mississippians. That night at the Co-Labor station, he entertained the crew with a few stories about the *Hee Haw* television show and some highlights of his career. He said:

It was a thrill to get back into show business, to make an album, and eight months later, it sold a million dollars' worth. It was a thrill that every album I have ever made has been a national hit. It was a thrill to me to be inducted into the world-famous Grand Ole Opry, and it was a thrill to be in the new Roy Rogers movie. I am not going to stand here and tell you that I'm not human enough to have been thrilled. But I want to go on record to say the greatest thrill I have ever had was when I was saved at Liberty, Mississippi. The preacher got up and said, "For all have sinned and come short of the glory of God." I said, "He ain't talking about everybody." And then the preacher said, "For the wages of sin is death." And I said, "My goodness; he means me." And I accepted Christ.

Team members and special guests visited the Co-Labor station every night of the crusade to add a little good-natured diversion. Just the evening before, Grady had told the story of the time he and Billy had been received by the Archbishop of Canterbury. The prelate, who was not terribly enamored of American evangelists, asked Graham how he and his party had traveled to Great Britain. Responding, Billy said that they had come over on the *Queen Elizabeth*, to which the Archbishop stiffly replied, "Well, you know, our Lord entered Jerusalem on a donkey." So Grady cried out, "Well, my Lord Archbishop, if you can tell me how to cross the Atlantic on an ass, I'll be glad to do so!"

That night at the Co-Labor station, I noticed a nice-looking couple sitting at a table near the back of the armory intently studying a batch of green cards. When I walked over and introduced myself, I discovered they were Judge and Mrs. Robert P. Sugg, he being an associate justice of the Mississippi Supreme Court. The couple had been recruited by their pastor, and were very delighted to be involved in the Co-Labor effort. I asked if sorting cards and checking addresses wasn't terribly dull work for an official of the state's highest judicial body. Judge Sugg replied, "I wouldn't miss it for anything in the world; this is a marvelous opportunity to participate in a great effort. I am the recipient of many blessings."

The Judge had taken some vacation time to help in the crusade, and Mrs. Sugg, who conducted a home prayer group, was also a crusade counselor. One evening, she talked with a black girl of fourteen who said, "I've been praying since I was ten for Billy Graham to come to Mississippi, and I'm so excited I don't know what to do!" The Judge, too, took considerable pride in the crusade's locale. He said, "As I have sat hearing Dr. Graham saying we are in Mississippi Memorial Stadium, I have been thrilled to realize that people around the world would know that he was in our state."

All reportorial objectivity aside, I was impressed by the sight of a high court judge sitting in a dank, hot room at 2:00 in the morning, thumbing through the Jackson telephone directory. I had to believe that such concern and dedication were directly related to Graham's appeal. Even though the Suggs, and probably all of the people sitting there in the armory, had never met the evangelist, they trusted, respected, and felt genuine affection for him. As Judge Sugg put it, "We don't know Billy Graham personally; but we know he is a tremendous influence for the witness of Christ, and we are very thankful for him."

LATE NIGHT DINNER PARTY

I left the Co-Labor station and made my way to Jim Carr's home, which was located in a quiet area in the northeastern part of the city. And as I entered the one-story, four-bedroom home, I heard the sounds of people who were relaxed and comfortable, and enjoying each other's company.

There were about forty guests present—Billy, Grady, T.W., Walter Smyth, Bev Shea, and several other team members and crusade officials. Also present were some close friends of the Carrs, and a few people Billy had asked the Carrs to invite, including the editor of the *Baptist Record,* the executive secretary of the Mississippi Baptist Convention, and several leaders of the 1952 Jackson Crusade.

Graham's presence at a strictly social function during the

course of a crusade was actually a break with his usual practice. But Martha Carr had been so pleasantly persistent in asking him to visit their home, and the Graham people had such great affection for Jim, who labored so long and hard to bring the crusade to Jackson, that Billy accepted the invitation. The dinner was a casual stand-up affair. A buffet table with hot chili, sandwiches, and salad had been laid out, and the guests circulated among the dining area, den, and playroom.

After he had eaten, Billy sat down and relaxed in a comfortable brown reclining chair. Dickie, the Carrs' six-year old, climbed onto Billy's lap, pointed his finger at him, and said, "I know you're a preacher. You jabber, jabber all the time." Dickie's remark cracked Billy up, and for a moment, all the strain and pressure of the awesome responsibilities he had undertaken during the very long and exhausting day were forgotten. An observer standing across the room whispered, "Out of the mouths of babes . . ."

Coffee was being served when Governor Waller, who had been at a late meeting at the state capitol, arrived. He and Graham exchanged warm greetings. Some of the guests talked of the evening's service, and marveled at the patience and fortitude of the crowd in staying put during the heavy rainfall.

Soon it was time to leave. After all, a new day, with all of its new challenges and opportunites, was almost upon us. As Billy was about to depart, he lifted Dickie up, who smiled and said, "Dr. Graham, you and me are buddies."

When all of the guests left, Jim Carr recalled a statement his wife had made during the time the crusade preparations were underway. She had said to him, "James, I've been so impressed with everybody I've met in the organization. I just hope when I meet Dr. Graham, I won't be disappointed." Jim knew that Martha wasn't disappointed in the least.

On the drive back to the Holiday Inn, Billy, Grady, and T.W. discussed the evening's service. Grady recalled a rainy night during their first Jackson Crusade, when R.G. LeTourneau, a businessman and staunch supporter of their work, was speaking on the subject of power. His presentation was interrupted by a bolt of lightning that knocked out the stadium's electrical system, and also sent a severe shock through his body. "I want power, but not *that* kind of power," LeTourneau had later quipped.

It was 11:30 when we pulled into the Holiday Inn driveway. Grady dropped off Billy and T.W., and then we continued on to the Hilton. Grady had to finalize arrangements there for an early morning breakfast meeting with some of the association's board members.

When Billy and T.W. walked into the hotel lobby, it was empty. The two old friends made their way into the elevator and ascended to their rooms. It was the end of one more evening in a lifetime of evenings that had been spent many miles from home and family.

TO REST

By the time Billy got back to his suite, the rain had ended and a half-moon was visible in the western sky. Tomorrow promised to be a fair day. Billy, who had been surrounded by people for the last sixteen hours, was now quite alone. Even though he could communicate with millions at that late hour simply by lifting the receiver of his telephone and dialing a news service, he would not do so. Why? Because he relished this time of privacy.

For the next seven hours he would just be Billy Graham, the man. He would be trying, like everyone else, to get through the night as best he could. And when he looked into the mirror, he would not see the immediately recognizable face of Billy Graham, the evangelist. Rather, he would see the reflection of a man who wondered whether he had done all he could for the cause that had motivated and shaped his life and brought him to this place.

He would not pause to consider what his coming to Jackson had accomplished. Nor would he ponder his tremendous impact on the city—how his presence there had changed lives; how people who had regarded one another as total strangers had begun to develop a sense of community; how blacks and whites in this seat of known racial animosity had, for the first time, visited one another's neighborhoods, churches, and homes. Rather, Billy Graham would think of those who did not come forward that night; of the refugees in distress on Guam; of the hundreds of people who have tried to reach him; of the masses who would eventually view the evening's televised service; of the meetings scheduled later that year in Texas and Europe and the Far East.

Billy Graham would think also of Ruth and the children and his close friends. And he would be assured, as he was every night of his life, that the God who brought him to the tent outside Charlotte, and who had sent him across the nation and the world to preach His Word, would continue to guide and bless him. And this uniquely authentic man would be satisfied and would rest.

Then tomorrow, Billy Graham would continue to run the race.

Billy Graham's message continues to offer hope and inspiration to people everywhere.

Epilogue

THE DRAMA OF BILLY GRAHAM'S LIFE, from North Carolina farm boy to world-famous personality, is the story of a man whose faith in the word of God has been instrumental in transforming the spiritual lives of millions of people everywhere.

A man of the South, Graham was able to transcend the racial and religious intolerance that characterized the world of his youth, and, in doing so, became a pathfinder in the cause of interracial and interreligious understanding. His early insistence on desegregated seating at crusades, his inclusion of Roman Catholics in crusade planning and implementation, and his outspoken opposition to anti-Semitism sent powerful messages to his core constituency.

During his more than five decades of ministry, Graham used developments in mass communication, such as television and, later, the Internet, to bring his message to the masses. He and his team also utilized modern travel methods, allowing them to reach greater numbers of people by crisscrossing the world in hours, rather than days.

The outreach of Graham's ministry has been unprecedented; he has addressed more people face-to-face than any other preacher (or politician, for that matter) in history; he has observed more people coming to Christ at his invitation than any of his evangelistic predecessors; and his ministry has led to the recruitment of thousands of people to full-time religious service as pastors, missionaries, and educators.

Further, the popularity of Graham's many best-selling books

contributed to the astounding growth of evangelical publishing—a development that prompted even secular publishing houses to establish religious divisions to compete with the growing number of religious publishers. Graham's *Hour of Decision* radio broadcast, as well as his frequent television specials, led to the expansion of the electronic church as other ministries sought to emulate his success, albeit some of them unethically.

As Graham communicated the Gospel through all practical outlets, he made the case for an enlightened evangelicalism, one that encompassed the historic truths, but with a compassionate and inclusive outreach, differing from the stilted and intolerant fundamentalism that had characterized earlier twentieth-century Bible-believing faith. Due in large part to Graham's efforts, by the end of the century, experts would add the term "evangelical" to Will Herberg's classic "Protestant, Catholic, Jew" formulation of the American religious experience.

As Graham's celebrity grew—along with his reputation for fiscal honesty and personal integrity—he became a national icon, an indispensable resource, who was called upon to offer prayers at inaugurations of presidents, as well as preside at their funerals. He also assisted the American people in dealing with national tragedies. The evangelist was asked to speak at the memorial service for the victims of the 1995 Oklahoma City bombing, and at the service held at the National Cathedral in Washington, DC, following the events of September 11, 2001. It was not that anyone expected Graham to say anything startlingly new or profound. Rather, his very presence at and participation in those memorials reassured the nation and the world that the American ship of state remained on course.

In looking back at Billy Graham's career, one is struck both by its longevity and by his ability for almost sixty years to have captured national and world attention. His success was due to a number of factors: to his having been free of any scandal; to his reputation for rectitude; and to his loving relationship with his wife, Ruth Bell Graham, with whom he had first fallen in love when both were students at Wheaton College.

In the last decades of his career, Graham was forced to go to extraordinary lengths to continue his crusade—now mission—schedule. One can only marvel at the self-discipline he mustered to continue to travel from stadium to stadium, despite the debilitating effects of age and ill-health and his concern for Ruth's well-being. And although the pace of Graham's activity slowed as he reached his octogenarian years, he was able to preside over the peaceful transition of the leadership of his organization to his son Franklin.

As his public career nears its end, Graham is still astonished at its success and even more amazed that God had raised him up for such a colossal enterprise. He well understood that there had been fellow students at Wheaton, as well as evangelistic colleagues in Youth for Christ, who had been better speakers, were more intellectually gifted, and had greater potential for outstanding Christian service. Throughout his life, Graham wondered why he had been chosen for the singular role he played in world evangelization. It was not that he doubted the will of God. Rather, from the human perspective, faced with the constant pressure of living up to his calling, he was on call twenty-four hours a day to play the cards he had been dealt. Thus, in essence, he was expected by believer and non-believer alike to be "Billy Graham," with all that it entailed. And he could accomplish that goal only by being assured of his own salvation through his allegiance to the veracity of the Scriptures, and in his belief in the power of prayer.

The Billy Graham the world thought it saw, the self-assured preacher who appeared to have the answers to human issues, was at root a work in progress—one who struggled every day to be the person he understood God had called him to be.

Graham has been a constant—the leader with whom America could most readily identify. In assessing the country's mood, Graham had not required the aid of pollsters; thousands of letters poured into his headquarters weekly, providing him with unusual insight into both the angst and aspirations of his fellow citizens. Thus, Graham has had his finger on the national pulse as no other religious figure before him. And, as he became more tolerant of racial, ethnic, and religious diversity, so too did the nation. If Billy Graham could embrace blacks, Catholics, Jews, and other minorities, then America had reason to follow along. To him, every individual—made in the image of God—was worthy of dignity and respect. Those individuals, however, were also in need of personal relationships with Christ.

Perhaps the most compelling reason for Graham's longevity as a public person is that no matter where he appeared, the evangelist never diluted his message. He has always been a soul-winner, a personal worker, who has had the opportunity to lead more people to Christ than any other person in history.

In reviewing Graham's sermons, broadcast and print interviews, and public speaking assignments outside the crusade settings, it is remarkable how often he has quoted from John 3:16: "For God so loved the world, that He gave His only begotten Son, that whosoever believeth in Him should not perish, but have everlasting life." Through this *New Testament* passage, which most succinctly and eloquently ties together the Gospel message, Graham has always offered his listeners a clear choice made in love, but also in urgency.

In each of his four messages at the 2002 Cincinnati Crusade, the evangelist repeated the words, "Cincinnati may never again have a moment like this." In a sense, he may have been describing his own situation—that he might never again stand before thousands of people, Bible in hand, insistently preaching the Good News. One thing we can recognize with certainty, however, is that Billy Graham has been true to his God and to his calling—and, most importantly, to himself.

Traveling with Billy Graham

Billy Graham's ministry has taken him across the nation and around the world. For over half a century, Mr. Graham has visited with and spoken to millions of people. What follows is a chronological listing of many of the places his crusades and missions, tours, rallies, and visits have led him.

1947

Grand Rapids, Michigan
Charlotte, North Carolina

1948

Augusta, Georgia
Modesto, California

1949

Miami, Florida
Baltimore, Maryland
Altoona, Pennsylvania
Los Angeles, California

1950

Boston, Massachusetts
Columbia, South Carolina

Tour—New England
  Portland, Maine

Waterville, Maine
Houlton, Maine
Springfield, Massachusetts
Providence, Rhode Island
Boston, Massachusetts
Hartford, Connecticut

Portland, Oregon
Minneapolis/St. Paul,
  Minnesota
Atlanta, Georgia

1951

Fort Worth, Texas
Shreveport, Louisiana
Cincinnati, Ohio
Memphis, Tennessee
Seattle, Washington
Hollywood, California
Greensboro, North Carolina

Raleigh, North Carolina

1952

Washington, DC
Houston, Texas
Jackson, Mississippi
Pittsburgh, Pennsylvania
Albuquerque, New Mexico

1953

Tour—Florida
  Tampa
  Miami
  Tallahassee
  St. Petersburg

Chattanooga, Tennessee
St. Louis, Missouri
Dallas, Texas

Tour—West Texas
  Tyler
  Amarillo
  Lubbock
  Wichita Falls

Syracuse, New York
Detroit, Michigan
Asheville, North Carolina

1954

London, England

Tour—Europe
  Helsinki, Finland
  Stockholm, Sweden
  Copenhagen, Denmark
  Amsterdam, The
    Netherlands

Frankfurt, West Germany
Dusseldorf, West Germany
Berlin, West Germany
Paris, France

Nashville, Tennessee
New Orleans, Louisiana

1955

Glasgow, Scotland

Tour—Scotland
  Aberdeen
  Inverness

London, England
Paris, France

Tour—Europe
  Zurich, Switzerland
  Geneve, Switzerland
  Stockholm, Sweden
  Copenhagen, Denmark
  Frankfurt, Germany
  Weisbaden, Germany
  Kaiserlautern, Germany
  Mannheim, Germany
  Stuttgart, Germany
  Nurnberg, Germany
  Dortmund, Germany
  U.S. Service Bases, West
    Germany
  Oslo, Norway
  Gothenburg, Sweden
  Aarhus, Denmark

Rotterdam, The Netherlands
Toronto, Ontario, Canada

1956

Tour—India
Bombay
Madras
Kottayam
Palmcottah
Dohnavur
New Delhi
Bangalore
Benares
Calcutta

Tour—Far East
Manila, Philippines
Hong Kong
Taipei, Formosa
Tokyo, Japan
Yokohama, Japan
Osaka, Japan
Seoul, Korea
Honolulu, Hawaii

Richmond, Virginia
Oklahoma City, Oklahoma
Louisville, Kentucky

1957

New York, New York

1958

Tour—Caribbean
Jamaica
Puerto Rico
Barbados
Trinidad
Panama
Costa Rica
Guatemala

Mexico City, Mexico
San Francisco, California
Sacramento, California
Fresno, California
Santa Barbara, California
Los Angeles, California
San Diego, California
Charlotte, North Carolina

1959

Tour—Australia/New Zealand
Melbourne
Canberra
Hobart
Launceston
Auckland
Wellington
Christchurch
Sydney
Perth
Adelaide
Brisbane

Little Rock, Arkansas
Wheaton, Illinois
Indianapolis, Indiana

1960

Tour—Africa
Monrovia, Liberia
Accra, Ghana
Kumasi, Ghana
Lagos, Nigeria
Kaduna, Nigeria
Ibadan, Nigeria
Enugu, Nigeria
Jos, Nigeria

Salisbury, Rhodesia
Bulawayo, South Rhodesia
Kitwe, North Rhodesia
Moshi, Tanganyika
Kisumu, Kenya
Usumbura, Ruanda-Urundi
Nairobi, Kenya
Brazzaville, Congo
Addis Ababa, Ethiopia
Dilla, Ethiopia
Cairo, Egypt

Tour—Israel
  Haifa
  Nazareth
  Jaffa
  Jerusalem

Washington, DC
Rio de Janeiro, Brazil

Tour—Europe
  Bern, Switzerland
  Zurich, Switzerland
  Basel, Switzerland
  Lausanne, Switzerland
  Essen, West Germany
  Hamburg, West Germany
  Berlin, West Germany

New York, New York (Spanish-
  American Crusade)

1961

Tour—Florida
  Jacksonville
  Orlando
  Clearwater
  St. Petersburg
  Tampa

Bradenton/Sarasota
Tallahassee
Gainesville
Miami
Cape Canaveral
West Palm Beach
Vero Beach
Bartow (Easter Sunrise
  Service - Peace River Park)
Boca Raton
Fort Lauderdale

Manchester, England
Glasgow, Scotland
Belfast, Ireland
Minneapolis/St. Paul,
  Minnesota
Philadelphia, Pennsylvania

1962

Tour—South America
  Maracaibo, Venezuela
  Barranquilla, Columbia
  Bogota, Columbia
  Cali, Columbia
  Quito, Ecuador
  Lima, Peru
  Santiago, Chile

Raleigh, North Carolina
Jacksonville, North Carolina
Chicago, Illinois
Seattle, Washington
Fresno, California
Huntsville, Alabama

Tour—South America
  Sao Paulo, Brazil
  Asuncion, Paraguay

Rosario, Argentina
Buenos Aires, Argentina
El Paso, Texas

1963
Tour—France
Montauban
Douai
Paris
Nancy
Toulouse
Lyon
Mulhouse

Los Angeles, California

1964
Birmingham, Alabama
Phoenix, Arizona
San Diego, California
Chicago, Illinois
Columbus, Ohio
Omaha, Nebraska
Boston, Massachusetts
Manchester, New Hampshire
Portland, Maine
Bangor, Maine
Providence, Rhode Island
Louisville, Kentucky

1965
Honolulu, Oahu, Hawaii
Kahului, Maui, Hawaii
Hilo, Hawaii
Lihue, Kauai, Hawaii
Dothan, Alabama
Tuscaloosa, Alabama

Auburn, Alabama
Tuskegee Institute, Alabama
Montgomery, Alabama
Copenhagen, Denmark
Vancouver, British Columbia,
   Canada
Seattle, Washington
Denver, Colorado
Houston, Texas

1966
Greenville, South Carolina
London, England
Berlin, West Germany

1967
Ponce, Puerto Rico
San Juan, Puerto Rico
Winnipeg, Manitoba, Canada
London, England
Turin, Italy
Zagreb, Yugoslavia
Toronto, Ontario, Canada
Kansas City, Missouri
Tokyo, Japan

1968
Brisbane, Australia
Sydney, Australia
Portland, Oregon
San Antonio, Texas
Pittsburgh, Pennsylvania

1969
Auckland, New Zealand
Dunedin, New Zealand

Melbourne, Australia
New York, New York
Anaheim, California

1970

Dortmund, West Germany
Knoxville, Tennessee
New York, New York
Baton Rouge, Louisiana

1971

Lexington, Kentucky
Chicago, Illinois
Oakland, California
Dallas/Fort Worth, Texas

1972

Charlotte, North Carolina
Birmingham, Alabama
Dallas, Texas
Cleveland, Ohio
Kohima, Nagaland, India

1973

Durban, South Africa
Johannesburg, South Africa
Seoul, South Korea
Atlanta, Georgia
Minneapolis/St. Paul,
    Minnesota
Raleigh, North Carolina
St. Louis, Missouri

1974

Phoenix, Arizona

Hollywood, California (25th
    Anniversary of first Los
    Angeles Crusade)
Rio de Janeiro, Brazil
Norfolk/Hampton, Virginia

1975

Albuquerque, New Mexico
Jackson, Mississippi
Brussels, Belgium
Lubbock, Texas
Taipei, Taiwan
Hong Kong

1976

Seattle, Washington
Williamsburg, Virginia
San Diego, California
Detroit, Michigan
Nairobi, Kenya

1977

Gothenburg, Sweden
Asheville, North Carolina
South Bend, Indiana

Tour—Hungary
    Budapest
    Debrecen
    Pecs

Cincinnati, Ohio
Manila, Philippines

Tour—India
    Calcutta
    Kottayam
    Madras

1978

Las Vegas, Nevada
Memphis, Tennessee
Toronto, Ontario, Canada
Kansas City, Missouri
Oslo, Norway
Stockholm, Sweden
Warsaw, Poland
Singapore

1979

Sao Paulo, Brazil
Tampa, Florida
Sydney, Australia
Nashville, Tennessee
Milwaukee, Wisconsin
Halifax, Nova Scotia,
    Canada

1980

Oxford, England
Cambridge, England
Indianapolis, Indiana
Edmonton, Alberta, Canada
Madurai, India

Tour—Japan
  Naha
  Okinawa
  Osaka
  Fukuoka
  Tokyo

Reno, Nevada
Las Vegas, Nevada

1981

Mexico City, Mexico

Villahermosa, Mexico
Boca Raton, Florida
Baltimore, Maryland
Calgary, Alberta, Canada
San Jose, California
Houston, Texas

1982

Blackpool, England

Tour—New England
  Providence, Rhode Island
  Burlington, Vermont
  Portland, Maine
  Springfield, Massachusetts
  Manchester, New
    Hampshire
  Hartford, Connecticut
  New Haven, Connecticut
  Boston, Massachusetts

New England Schools
  Yale University–New Haven,
    Connecticut
  Harvard University–
    Cambridge, Massachusetts
  Boston College–Newton,
    Massachusetts
  Massachusetts Institute of
    Technology–Cambridge,
    Massachusetts
  Dartmouth College–
    Hanover, New
    Hampshire
  Northeastern University–
    Boston, Massachusetts
  University of Massachusetts–
    Amherst, Massachusetts

Gordon-Conwell Seminary–
South Hamilton,
Massachusetts

New Orleans, Louisiana

Boise, Idaho

Spokane, Washington

Chapel Hill, North Carolina

**Tour—German Democratic
Republic**
Wittenberg
Dresden (Saxony)
Gorlitz
Stendal
Stralsund
Berlin

Tour—Czechoslovakia
Bratislava
Brno
Prague

Nassau, Bahamas

1983

Orlando, Florida
Tacoma, Washington
Sacramento, California
Oklahoma City, Oklahoma

1984

Anchorage, Alaska

Tour—England
Bristol
Sunderland
Norwich
Birmingham
Liverpool

Ipswich

Seoul, South Korea

**Tour—Union of Soviet
Socialist Republics**
Moscow, Russia
Leningrad, Russia
Tallinn, Estonia
Novosibirsk, Siberia

Vancouver, British Columbia,
Canada

1985

Fort Lauderdale, Florida
Hartford, Connecticut
Sheffield, England
Anaheim, California

Tour—Romania/Hungary
Timisoara
Sibiu
Suceava
Cluj-Napoca
Oradea
Arad
Bucharest
Pecs
Budapest

1986

Washington, DC
Paris, France
Tallahassee, Florida

1987

Columbia, South Carolina
Cheyenne, Wyoming

Fargo, North Dakota
Billings, Montana
Sioux Falls, South Dakota
Denver, Colorado
Helsinki, Finland

1988

**Tour—People's Republic
of China**
Beijing
Nanjing
Huaiyin
Shanghai
Guangzhou

**Tour—Union of Soviet
Socialist Republics**
Zagorsk, Russia
Moscow, Russia
Kiev, Ukraine

Buffalo, New York
Rochester, New York
Hamilton, Ontario, Canada

1989

Syracuse, New York
London, England
Budapest, Hungary
Little Rock, Arkansas

1990

Berlin, West Germany
Montreal, Quebec, Canada
Albany, New York
Uniondale, Long Island,
    New York
Hong Kong

1991

Tacoma, Washington
Seattle, Washington

Tour—Scotland
Edinburgh
Aberdeen
Glasgow

East Rutherford, New Jersey
New York, New York
    (Central Park)
Buenos Aires, Argentina

1992

Pyongyang, North Korea
Philadelphia, Pennsylvania
Portland, Oregon
Moscow, Russia

1993

Essen, Germany
Pittsburgh, Pennsylvania
Columbus, Ohio

1994

Tokyo, Japan
Beijing, People's Republic
    of China
Pyongyang, North Korea
Cleveland, Ohio
Atlanta, Georgia

1995

San Juan, Puerto Rico
Toronto, Ontario, Canada
Sacramento, California

1996

Minneapolis/St. Paul,
  Minnesota
Charlotte, North Carolina

1997

San Antonio, Texas
San Jose, California
San Francisco, California
Oakland, California

1998

Albuquerque, New Mexico
Ottawa, Ontario, Canada
Tampa, Florida

1999

Indianapolis, Indiana
St. Louis, Missouri

2000

Nashville, Tennessee
Jacksonville, Florida

2001

Louisville, Kentucky
Fresno, California

2002

Cincinnati, Ohio
Dallas/Fort Worth, Texas

2003

San Diego, California
Oklahoma City, Oklahoma

Books by
Billy Graham

Calling Youth to Christ (1947)

I Saw Your Sons at War (1953)

Peace With God (1953)

Freedom from the Seven Deadly Sins (1955)

The Secret of Happiness (1955)

Billy Graham Talks to Teenagers (1958)

My Answer (1960)

Billy Graham Answers Your Questions (1960)

World Aflame (1965)

The Challenge (1969)

The Jesus Generation (1971)

Angels: God's Secret Agents (1975)

How to Be Born Again (1977)

The Holy Spirit (1978)

Till Armageddon (1981)

*Approaching Hoofbeats: The Four Horsemen
of the Apocalypse* (1983)

A Biblical Standard for Evangelists (1984)

Unto the Hills (1986)

Facing Death and the Life After (1987)

Answers to Life's Problems (1988)

Hope for the Troubled Heart (1991)

Storm Warning (1992)

Just As I Am (1997)

Hope for Each Day (2002)

Contact Information

To learn more about Billy Graham and the Billy Graham Evangelistic Association, log onto the BGEA website—www.bgea.org—or contact the association:

BY PHONE

Local: 1-612-338-0500

Toll-Free (within the United States or Canada):
1-877-2GRAHAM (1-877-247-2426)

Call between 7 AM and 7 PM Central Time, Monday through Friday.

BY MAIL

NORTH AMERICAN OFFICES

Minneapolis Headquarters
BGEA
PO Box 779
Minneapolis, MN 55440

Charlotte Transition Office
BGEA
PO Box 1270
Charlotte, NC 28201

INTERNATIONAL OFFICES

Australia
Billy Graham Evangelistic
   Assoc., Ltd.
PO Box 4807 GPO
Sydney NSW 2001
Australia

Canada
BGEA of Canada
PO Box 841 Station Main
Winnipeg, MB R3C 2R3
Canada
Phone: (204) 943-0529
Fax: (204) 943-7407

France
Institut Biblique
85 Avenue de Cherbourg
78740 Vaux-sur-Siene
France

Germany
Geschenke der Hoffnung e.V.
Haynauer. Str. 72 a
12249 Berlin
Germany
Phone: (+49-30) 7 68 83-5 50
Fax: (+49-30) 7 68 83-3 33

New Zealand
BGEA
PO Box 870
Auckland, New Zealand

Spain
C/. Mequinenza 20
28022 Madrid
Spain
Phone: (34-91) 742-7911

United Kingdom
Billy Graham Evangelistic
    Assoc., Ltd.
PO Box 2032
Woodford Green
Essex IG9 5AP
England
Phone: 020 8559 0342
Fax: 020 8502 9062

Index

A

Alexander, Shaun, 14
Alexandrovich, Rivka, 118
Alexandrovich, Ruth, 118, 119
Ali, Muhammad, 5
Allen, Charles L., 89
American Jewish Committee, 36, 118, 134, 141
Angels, 61, 71,

B

Bader, Jesse, 42
Baily, Don, 40, 48, 50–51, 121, 122, 127, 132, 163, 164
Baily, Tom, 73
Baptist Record, 94, 166
Barrows, Billie, 49, 85
Barrows, Cliff, 14, 15, 28, 48, 49, 71, 76, 80, 84, 85–86, 122, 142, 143–144, 164
Bell, L. Nelson, 26, 28, 36, 48, 75
Bell, Ralph, 11, 111
Bellah, Robert, 115
Ben Dov, David, 133

Ben Yaacov, Yissachar, 136, 137
Bennett, Walter, 52
Berlin Congress on Evangelism, 46
Berry, Lowell, 87–88, 94
Beversluis, Claire, 121
BGEA. *See* Billy Graham Evangelistic Association.
Billy Graham Evangelistic Association (BGEA), 8
  origin and early growth of, 30, 52, 57–58
  and Emergency Relief Fund, 130–132, 145
  and financial management of, 42–43, 58
  and handling of correspondence, 53
  and original team, 48–49
  theological beliefs of, 10
  See also Graham Team.
Blue Ridge Broadcasting Corporation, 51–52
Bob Jones College, 26, 47, 56
Bowman, S.L., 109

"Boycott Cincinnati," 5
Brown, Bill, 65
Brown, Reese, 25
Bryant, Ellen, 158–159
Bryant, Tom, 158–159
Burgin, Corinne, 67
Burgin, George, 67
Bush, George W., 61
Bush, Laura, 5
Butler, Judy, 157

C

Carr, Dickie, 167
Carr, Jim, 79, 80, 81, 82, 83–84, 163, 166–167
Carr, Martha, 80, 167
Carter, June, 76, 121, 129–130, 146–147, 163
Cash, Johnny, 76, 97, 121, 127, 129–130, 146–147, 163
Chafin, Kenneth, 87, 88, 89, 90, 91, 129
Chicago Sun Times, 31
Christian Motorcycle Association, 22
Christianity Today, 47, 87
Churchill, Winston, 30
Cincinnati, Ohio, about, 4–6
Cincinnati Enquirer, 6
Cincinnati Herald, 5
Cincinnati Mission (2002)
    advertising of, 12–13
    Co-Labor activity of, 22
    effort behind, 4

Graham's sermon for, 15–20
    and opening night program, 14–21
    outreach programs of, 7, 10–11
    preparing for, 7–14
Clower, Jerry, 164–165
Co-Labor activity, 22, 164–166
Concerned Clergy, 6
Cooperative Evangelism, 93
Crusades. *See* Missions/Crusades.
Cushing, Larry, 159
Cushing, Laura, 158

D

Decision magazine, 20, 63, 78, 82, 87, 98, 157
Demopolis, Peter, 136
Dienert, Fred, 52
Dodds, Gil, 125

E

East Gate Ministries International, 33
"Ecumenicity" and Billy Graham, 43–46
Edman, V. Raymond, 47
Edwards, Jonathan, 44, 152
Eisenhower, Dwight D., 61
Emergency Relief Fund, 130–132, 146
Evangelism, School of. *See* School of Evangelism.
Evers, Medgar, 108

F

Ferm, Robert D., 87
Finney, Charles, 44
Fisher, Lee, 122
Florida Bible Institute, 26, 28, 47, 56, 66
Ford, Gerald, 62, 69, 105
Franklin, Bill C., 73, 159–160
Friend-to-Friend program, 12, 13
Fuller, Charles E., 152

G

Goldwater, Barry, 53, 121
Gomez, Joyce, 97
Graham, Ann, 32
Graham, Billy
    and beliefs on Israel's future, 141
    and beliefs on salvation of man, 95–96
    and beliefs on Second Coming of Christ, 69–70, 132
    as businessman, 58
    and concerns over Middle East, 120, 132
    and concerns over Southeast Asia, 103–105
    and cooperative evangelism, 93–94
    and correspondence, 53–54
    critics of, 54–55, 115
    and "ecumenicity," 42–46, 56
    family of, 25, 32–33
    and Jewish community, 31, 64, 118, 139–140
    and the media, 41–42, 51
    and overview of life, 25–33
    physical appearance of, 39
    and racial accord and integration, 92–93, 106, 108–110, 111–112
    reading habits of, 60, 79
    and relationship with presidents, 61–62
    and sermon preparation, 54–55, 59
    and speaking at public events, 62
    and television ministry, 31–32
    and treatment of staff, 49–50
    and visit to Israel, 133–142
    and women's rights, 68–69
    work ethic of, 66–67
    and world evangelism, 22, 32
    as writer, 60–61, 71
Graham, Bunny, 32–33, 58–59
Graham, Franklin, 8, 14–15, 17, 33
Graham, Gigi, 32
Graham, Ned, 33
Graham, Ruth Bell, 26, 32, 46–48, 52, 58–59, 60, 66, 67–68, 69, 71–72, 135, 169
Graham Team, 11, 42, 48–49, 74, 75, 115–117, 121
Greentree, Florence, 144
Gulag Archipelago, 60

Gunn, Peck, 121

Gustafson, Roy, 133

H

Hadassah Hospital, 136, 141–142

Ham, Mordechai, 25, 26

Haymaker, Wills, 29

Hearst, William Randolph, 29, 99

Herndon, Sarah, 160–161

Hiding Place, The, 63–64, 65

Hill, E.V., 105–111, 131

His Land, 31, 140

Honor America Day, 115

Hope, Bob, 115

Horner, George, 112

Hour of Decision, 30, 40, 51, 52, 57, 63, 75, 85, 114, 142

Humphrey, Hubert, 60

Huston, Sterling, 49, 81, 113–114, 115, 116, 127, 129

I

Inquirers

    at Cincinnati Crusade, 20–21

    follow-up provisions for, 98, 164

    at Jackson Crusade, 156–162

Israel, trip to, 133–142

J

Jackson, Basil, 89

Jackson, Henry, 60

Jackson Crusade (1975), 40, 45, 50, 51, 54

budget for, 81–82

Co-Labor activity of, 164–166

committee work for, 81–84,

and dinner party, 166–167

evening service of, 143–162

genesis of, 79–81

and Graham at crusade office, 96–97

and Graham at Governor's Prayer Breakfast, 74, 77–78

and Graham at School of Evangelism, 91–96

and Graham's invitation to come forward, 154–155

and Graham's sermon, 148–154

and response to Graham's invitation, 154–162

Johnson, Harold, 129

Johnson, Lyndon, 61, 103

Johnson, Torrey, 27

Jones, Bob, 29

Jones, Bob, Jr., 43

Jones, Davis, 49

Jones, Howard, 49, 111, 112, 122, 130–131, 132

Jones, Mrs. Howard, 50

K

Kennedy, John F., 61, 103

"Key '73," 115

King, Martin Luther, 112

Kissinger, Henry, 118

Kolleck, Teddy, 136, 137, 138, 139

L

Landry, Tom, 84

Larson, Roy, 31

Lausanne Conference, 46

LeTourneau, R.G., 167–168

Lewis, Hobart, 115

Lindsay, Bob, 141

Lindsell, Harold, 47, 55–56, 66, 87, 89, 120, 127, 132, 152

Little, Paul, 89

Los Angeles tent meetings (1949), 28, 99

"Love in Action" program, 10–11

Luce, Henry, 29

Lynch, Damon, Jr., 9–10

M

Man in Black, 147

Mayaguez, seizing of, 123, 126, 127, 132, 144, 156

McGovern, George, 60

McIntyre, Carl, 43

McLaughlin, John, 99

Mears, Henrietta, 28

Meir, Golda, 134–135

Meredith, James, 108

Mission/Crusades
  and executive committee, 9–10
  and director's role, 9
  outreach programs of, 10–11
  preparing for, 8–14
  purpose of, 8–9
  See also Co-Labor activity; Friend-to-Friend program; School of Evangelism; Share Partners.

Montreat, North Carolina, 32, 33, 35, 36, 54

Montreat-Anderson College, 35, 55

Montreat Conference Center, 35, 68

Moody, Dwight Lyman, 44

Moore, Arthur, 55

Morrison's Cafeteria, 73, 101

Moyers, Bill, 99

Muñoz, Anthony, 9, 14

My Answer, 58

My Life, 135

N

National Underground Railroad Freedom Center, 5, 15

New York Times, The, 60, 62

Newton, John, 131

Nixon, Richard, 61–62, 103, 104, 111, 115, 118, 134

Northwestern Schools, 27, 28, 57

O

Okengea, Harold John, 29

Oklahoma City bombing, 62

O'Neal, Rousseau, 6

Operation Andrew, 83. *See also* Friend-to-Friend program.

Outreach programs, 10–11

P

Palm, Roger, 157

Patterson, Donald, 109

Paulson, Bob, 20

Pearson, Jim, 157

Pentagon, attack on, 62

Phillips, Tom, 22

Pollard, Dr., 94

Pride, Herman, 109

R

Rabin, Leah, 140

Rabin, Yitzhak, 133, 140–141

Reznikoff, Bernard, 141

Rice, John R., 43

Riggs, Charlie, 22, 82–83, 89, 94, 97, 101, 102, 122, 163, 164

Riley, William B., 27–28

Rogers, Linda May, 73, 161–162

Ross, Larry, 7

S

Samaritan's Purse, 14, 17, 33

Sanders, Norman, 111

School of Evangelism, 78, 86–89, 129

Share Partners, 82

Sharpton, Al, 5

Shea, George Beverly, 14, 15, 27, 28, 48, 49, 85, 144, 148, 166

Smith, Gypsy, 29

Smyth, Walter, 81, 122, 133, 141, 166

Solzhenitsyn, Alexander, 60

Songs in the Night, 27

Spellman, Francis Cardinal, 103–104

Spurgeon, Charles Haddon, 152

Sugg, Judge Robert P., 165–166

Sugg, Mrs. Robert, 165–166

T

Taft, Bob, 8

Tannenbaum, Marc, 134

ten Boom, Betsy, 64

ten Boom, Corrie, 63, 64

Till, Emmett, 108

Times-Picayune, 92

Truman, Harry, 61

W

Wallace, Clarence, 6

Waller, Bill, 77, 78, 167

Washington Post, The, 41, 43, 60

Waters, Ethel, 128–129

Western Wall, visit to, 137–138

Wheatley, Carol, 73, 158

Wheatley, Jimmy, 73, 158

Wheaton College, 26, 47, 56, 68, 72, 112

Wheeler, Steven K., 5

White, Hugh, 112

Wilberforce, William, 131

Williams, John, 111

Wills, Stephanie, 37, 38, 53, 58, 78, 79, 85

Wilson, George, 28, 48–49, 57–58, 62–63

Wilson, Grady, 26, 28, 37, 48, 49, 69, 75–76, 78, 79, 80, 85, 89, 105, 119, 122, 125–126, 127, 133, 141, 143, 155, 163, 166, 168

Wilson, T.W., 26, 37–38, 39, 40, 41, 48, 50, 63, 65, 67–71, 72, 75, 76, 103, 105, 122, 125–126, 127, 130, 143, 163, 166

Wirt, Sherwood, 78–79, 87, 156

World Medical Missions, 14–15, 33

World Trade Center, attack on, 62

World Wide Pictures, 31, 38, 57, 63, 65, 140, 141

Wright, John, 31

Y

Youth for Christ, 15, 27, 48, 49, 57, 113

AS A MAN DOES

Morning and Evening Thoughts
James Allen

One of the first great modern writers of motivational and inspirational books, James Allen has influenced millions of people through books like *As a Man Thinketh*. In the same way, *As a Man Does: Morning and Evening Thoughts* presents beautiful and insightful meditations to feed the mind and soul.

In each of the sixty-two meditations—one for each morning and each evening of the month—Allen offers spiritual jewels of wisdom, reflecting the deepest experiences of the heart. Whether you are familiar with the writings of James Allen or you have yet to read any of his books, this beautiful volume is sure to move you, console you, and inspire you—every morning and every evening of your life.

$8.95 • 144 pages • 5.5 x 8.5-inch quality paperback • 2-color • Inspiration/Religion • ISBN 0-7570-0018-5

AS A MAN THINKETH

Tending the Garden of the Mind
by James Allen

Here is the classic James Allen work that has inspired millions around the world to change their lives for the better. For nearly a hundred years, Allen's words of positive thinking have provided the foundation for many of today's motivational leaders, including Norman Vincent Peale, Dale Carnegie, and Billy Graham. In this concise work, Allen offers a simple yet elegant message about the innate power of control we all possess. *As a Man Thinketh* provides the means to gain confidence in ourselves, to take charge of the way we perceive things, and to reshape who we are to meet and conquer life's inevitable challenges.

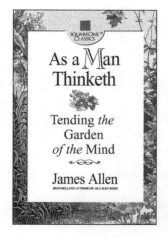

This attractive two-color edition of *As a Man Thinketh* can make a wonderful gift to be read and reread. For those who are interested in other works by James Allen, check his other insightful titles in the SquareOne Classics series.

$8.95 • 64 pages • 5.5x 8.5-inch quality paperback • 2-Color • Inspiration/Religion • ISBN 0-7570-0077-0

THE LIFE TRIUMPHANT
Mastering the Heart and Mind
James Allen

"In the midst of the world, darkened with many sins and many sorrows, in which the majority live, there abides another world, lighted up with shining virtues and unpolluted joy."

Blending spirituality with the power of positive thinking, inspirational author James Allen provides a simple blueprint for achieving a life filled with joy—joy of freedom, of faith, and of virtue. *The Life Triumphant* offers ten thoughtful essays in which Allen presents insightful advice on overcoming life's challenges by drawing on one's inner strength. Some of the topics discussed in this work include "Faith and Courage," "Self-Control and Happiness," "Calmness and Repose," and "Energy and Power."

$8.95 • 96 pages • 5.5 x 8.5-inch quality paperback • 2-color • Inspiration/Religion • ISBN 0-7570-0084-3

LIGHT ON LIFE'S DIFFICULTIES
Illuminating the Paths Ahead
James Allen

James Allen is considered to be one of the first great modern writers of motivational and inspirational books. Today, his work *As a Man Thinketh* continues to influence millions around the world. In the same way, this newly discovered classic, *Light on Life's Difficulties,* offers twenty-three beautiful and insightful essays. Readers will find that each essay contains both the force of truth and the blessing of comfort.

In a time of crisis, *Light on Life's Difficulties* offers clear direction to those on a search for personal truths. In Allen's own words, "This book is intended to be a strong and kindly companion, as well as a source of spiritual renewal and inspiration. It will help its readers transform themselves into the ideal characters they would wish to be."

Light on Life's Difficulties is designed to shed light on those areas of our lives that we have become uncertain about—areas such as spirituality, self-control, individual liberty, war and peace, sorrow, and so much more. Although written almost one hundred years ago, the power of Allen's words can and will illuminate the road ahead for so many of us.

$8.95 • 128 pages • 5.5 x 8.5-inch quality paperback • 2-color • Inspiration/Religion • ISBN 0-7570-0040-1

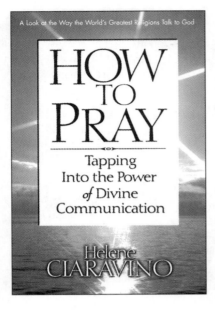

HOW TO PRAY
Tapping Into the Power of Divine Communication
Helene Ciaravino

The power of prayer is real. It can heal illness, win battles, and move personal mountains. Cultures and religions throughout the world use their own individual systems of divine communication for comfort, serenity, guidance, and more. *How to Pray* was written for everyone who wants to learn more about this universal practice.

How to Pray begins by widening your perspective on prayer through several intriguing definitions. It then discusses the many scientific studies that have validated the power of prayer, and—to shine a light on any roadblocks that may be hindering you—it discusses common reasons why some people don't pray. Part Two examines the history and prayer techniques of four great traditions: Judaism, Christianity, Islam, and Buddhism. In these chapters, you'll learn about the beliefs, practices, and individual prayers that have been revered for centuries. Part Three focuses on the development of your own personal prayer life, first by explaining some easy ways in which you can make your practice of prayer more effective and fulfilling, and then by exploring the challenges of prayer—from seemingly unanswered prayers and spiritual dry spells, to the joyful task of making your whole day a prayer. Finally, a useful resource directory suggests books and websites that provide further information.

$13.95 • 264 pages • 6 x 9-inch quality paperback • Inspiration/Self-Help • ISBN 0-7570-0012-6